MAN MEETS DOG

KONRAD LORENZ

MAN MEETS DOG

TRANSLATED BY MARJORIE KERR WILSON
ILLUSTRATED BY ANNIE EISENMENGER
AND THE AUTHOR

METHUEN & CO. LTD
LONDON

This translation from the German by Marjorie Kerr Wilson
First published in 1954 *by*
Methuen & Co Ltd
Reprinted six times
Reprinted 1977
First published in paperback in 1979

ISBN 0 416 57320 7 *(hardback)*
ISBN 0 416 72350 0 *(paperback)*

Printed in Great Britain at the
University Press, Cambridge

CONTENTS

INTRODUCTION:

MAN AND THE DOMESTIC ANIMALS

> *Or by necessity constrained, they live*
> *Dependent upon Man; those in his fields,*
> *These at his crib, and some beneath his roof.*
> *They prove too often at how dear a rate*
> *He sells protection.*
>
> COWPER: *The Winter Walk at Noon*

TO-DAY for breakfast I ate some fried bread and sausage. Both the sausage and the lard that the bread was fried in came from a pig that I used to know as a dear little piglet. Once that stage was over to save my conscience from conflict, I meticulously avoided any further acquaintance with that pig. I should probably only eat animals up to the mental level of fish or, at the most, frogs, if I were obliged to kill them myself. It is, of course, hypocritical to avoid, in this way, the moral responsibility for the murder. But, in any case, the attitude of a human being to the animals which he rears for food is a somewhat contradictory one. In the case of farmers, who follow a certain age-old tradition, the relation of man to beast is determined by a line of conduct of an almost ritual kind which becomes so much a matter of course as to relieve him of any moral responsibility or feeling of compunction. But for the man who is engaged professionally in research into the animal mind which, in its inmost workings, so much resembles our own, the matter assumes an entirely different aspect. For him, the slaughtering of a farm animal is something infinitely worse than the shooting of game. The hunter does not know the latter personally or, at least, not so intimately as the farmer does the domestic animal and, above all, the game animal recognizes the danger it is in. Morally it is much worse to wring the neck of a tame goose which approaches one confidently to take food from one's hand than it is, at the expense of some physical effort and a great deal of patience, to shoot a wild goose which is fully conscious of its danger and, moreover, has a good chance of eluding it. Almost more questionable than the relations of man to the animals which he honestly consumes and which, up to the time of their unexpected and usually quick death, lead an easy and comfortable life, is his attitude towards those which he uses for other purposes. The fate of the horse, which, with advancing years, leads an ever more tragic existence, is too pitiable to dwell upon. And the coldbloodedness with which calves are slaughtered, and even the cow herself when, milked to the last drop, she can no longer 'pay her way', is one of the less pleasant aspects of the association between man and the domestic animals.

It is only from a very wide biological viewpoint which considers not the individual but the species as a whole, that the connection between man and animals can be looked upon as a mutual advantage, a 'symbiosis'. One might say that the species, Horse, Cow, Sheep etc. might in some measure welcome their domestication since their wild progenitors,

unable to exist in civilized countries, became extinct
long ago.

Another feature which exculpates man to some
extent is the fact that he is bound by no agreement,
by no contract with the animals in question, to treat
them as anything but enemies which he has taken
prisoner. Even highly civilized peoples in the eras
before Christ were accustomed to treat their
prisoners no better than domestic animals. The
North American Indians used to martyr them and
the Papuans eat them even to-day with excellent
appetite and with much less moral compunction
than I felt this morning on eating that sausage.

Only two animals have entered the human household otherwise than as prisoners and become
domesticated by other means than those of enforced
servitude: the dog and the cat. Two things they have
in common, namely, that both belong to the order
of carnivores and both serve man in their capacity
of hunters. In all other characteristics, above all, in
the manner of their association with man, they are
as different as the night from the day. There is no
domestic animal which has so radically altered its
whole way of living, indeed its whole sphere of
interests, that has become domestic in so true a sense
as the dog: and there is no animal that, in the course
of its century-old association with man, has altered
so little as the cat. There is some truth in the
assertion that the cat, with the exception of a few
luxury breeds, such as Angoras, Persians and Siamese, is no domestic animal but a completely wild
being. Maintaining its full independence it has taken
up its abode in the houses and outhouses of man, for
the simple reason that there are more mice there
than elsewhere. The whole charm of the dog lies in
the depth of the friendship and the strength of the

spiritual ties with which he has bound himself to man, but the appeal of the cat lies in the very fact that she has formed no close bond with him, that she has the uncompromising independence of a tiger or a leopard while she is hunting in his stables and barns; that she still remains mysterious and remote when she is rubbing herself gently against the legs of her mistress or purring contentedly in front of the fire. The purring cat is, for me, a symbol of the hearthside and the hidden security which it stands for. I should no more like to be without a cat in my home than to be without the dog that trots behind me in field or street. Since my earliest youth I have always had dogs and cats about me, and it is about them that I shall talk in this book. Business-like friends have advised me to write a dog-book and a cat-book separately, because dog-lovers often dislike cats and cat-lovers frequently abhor dogs. But I consider it the finest test of genuine love and understanding of animals if a person has sympathies for both these creatures, and can appreciate in each its own special virtues.

To all those who love and understand dogs and cats alike I dedicate this little book.

I. HOW IT MAY HAVE STARTED

Some show that nice sagacity of smell,
And read with such discernment in the port
And figure of the man, his secret aim
That oft we owe our safety to a skill
We could not teach and must despair to learn.

COWPER

THROUGH the tall grass of the plain a little group of people makes its way, an unclothed, uncivilized band. They are certainly human beings like ourselves, their build no different from that of present-day man. In their hands they carry bone-tipped spears, some even have bows and arrows, but in their behaviour there is something which would be foreign even to present-day savages of the lowest cultural type, and which would strike a modern observer as being an animal trait. These men are no lords of creation that look fearlessly out into the world; instead, their dark eyes move to and fro restlessly as they turn their heads, glancing from time to time fearfully over their shoulders. They remind one of deer, hunted animals that must always be watchful. They give wide berth to bushes and the taller vegetation of the steppes which may easily shelter a large beast of prey, and, as on one occasion, a big antelope breaks cover with a loud rustling, they start nervously, hastily adjusting their spears for action. The next moment recognizing the harmlessness of the animal, their fear gives place to relieved but excited chatter and finally to hilarious laughter. But this cheerful mood soon subsides: the band is downcast and with good reason. In the course of the last month, they have been forced by stronger, more populous tribes, to relinquish their original hunting grounds for the plains of the West, a country which they do not know and where large beasts of prey are much more prevalent than in the abandoned territory. The knowing old hunter who was their leader lost his life a few weeks ago; he was wounded by a sabre-toothed tiger which tried one night to steal a young girl from the band. In a fever of excitement, all the men set their spears at the tiger, the leader at their head, but unluckily it was he that received the brunt of its attack. The girl was already dead and the leader died of his wounds the next day. The fact that the tiger also died a week later of peritonitis caused by a spear wound in his abdomen was of small direct advantage to the little band of people. This now consisted of but five grown men, the rest being women and children, and five men are not enough to beat off the attacks of a large beast of prey. Nor is the man who has assumed the leadership so endowed with experience and muscle-power as was the former leader. But his eyes are brighter and his forehead higher and more arched than that of the other. The depleted group suffers most from lack of sleep. In their own territory they used to sleep round the fire and, moreover, they possessed a guard of which, till now, they were unaware. The jackals that followed in the tracks of the human hordes, scavenging the refuse from slaughtered animals, surrounded their camp at night in a close circle. No feelings of friendship united the humans with their troublesome followers. Missiles greeted every jackal that dared approach too near the fire, and occasionally an arrow was aimed at them, though it was seldom that one was wasted on such unappetising creatures.

Even to-day, in the eyes of many peoples, the dog is still marked out as an unclean animal in consequence of his disreputable ancestors. Nevertheless, the jackals were a definite help to the human beings whose footsteps they followed: to some extent, they saved them the trouble of setting a watch, since the clamour they set up on the approach of a beast of prey announced from afar the appearance of the marauder.

These primitive human beings, careless and un-thinking, were unaware of this usefulness of their four-legged retinue; but now that it was missing, the uncanny stillness around the camp was so sinister that even those who were not entrusted with the watch hardly dared to close an eye; and this proved most exhausting, since their vigilance was already overtaxed owing to the small number of able-bodied men that their band included. And so the little company, tired and nervous and thoroughly disconsolate, pursued its way, jumping at every sound and seizing its weapons, and now very seldom bursting into guffaws when the alarm proved to be a false one. At the approach of evening, the dread of the coming night began to weigh heavy on every mind; they were obsessed by that fear of the unknown which, engraved in bygone eras into the convolutions of our brain, renders even to-day the darkness of night a source of terror to the child and, to the adult, the symbol of all things evil. This is an age-old memory of the time when the powers of darkness, in the form of flesh-eating beasts of prey, sprang out of the night upon human beings. For our forefathers the night must indeed have held unlimited terrors.

The silent group of people presses closer together and begins searching for a place far from any bushy cover, where they will be safe from the attack of predatory beasts. Here, by a slow and tiresome procedure, they will light their camp fire and roast and divide the meagre spoils of the day. The repast consists to-day of the already 'high' remains of a wild boar, the leavings from the meal of the sabre-toothed tiger, from which the men had driven off, after a struggle, a pack of hyena dogs. Such a mutilated carcase would hardly seem appetising to us but the members of the band cast hungry looks at their leader who is carrying the half-eaten skeleton himself in order to save any less responsible person from temptation. Suddenly the footsteps of the band halt as if at an order. All heads are turned in the direction whence they have come and, like a herd of startled deer, they all focus their senses in that one direction. They have heard a sound, the call of an animal which, strangely enough, brings no threat with it as most animal calls do: for only the hunting animal gives tongue—the hunted have long ago learned to be silent. But this sound seems to the wanderers like a message from home, a reminder of happier and less dangerous times, for it is the howl of a jackal. It almost seems as though the band, in its child-like, almost ape-like impulsiveness, will hurry back in the direction whence the howling proceeds. Strangely moved, they stand in anticipation. Then suddenly the young leader with the high forehead does something remarkable and, to the others, inexplicable: he throws the carcase to the ground and begins to rip off a large piece of skin to which some flesh still adheres. Some young members of the band, thinking that a meal is about to be distributed, come close, but with furrowed brow, the leader repulses them with a deep

grunt of anger. Leaving the detached pieces of meat
on the ground, he picks up the rest of the carcase and
gives the signal for marching. They have hardly
advanced a few steps when the man who stands
nearest the leader in rank, and who is physically
stronger though mentally less active, challenges him,
indicating with his eyes and with head movements—
not, as we would do it, with the hands—the abandoned piece of meat. The leader reproaches him and
presses onward. After another ten yards, the second
man falls back and moves towards the meat. The
leader, throwing his booty into the grass, pursues
him and, as the other raises the reeking flesh to his
mouth, he rams his shoulder against him causing him
to totter sideways. For a few seconds the two face
each other threateningly, their foreheads puckered,
their faces distorted with rage; then the second man
drops his eyes and, muttering, follows the group,
which is now once more in motion.

Not a man is conscious that he has just witnessed
an epoch-making episode, a stroke of genius whose
meaning in world history is greater than that of the
fall of Troy or the discovery of gunpowder. Even the
high-browed leader himself does not know it. He
acted on impulse, hardly realizing that the motive for
his action was the wish to have the jackals near him.
He had instinctively and rightly calculated that since
the wind was blowing against them it was bound to
waft the scent of the meat into the nostrils of the howling jackals. The band moves on, but still no open
space is to be found, which could offer them a safe
camping place. After a few hundred yards, the leader
repeats his strange action whereupon a loud protest is
raised by the other men. The third time he repeats it
something like a revolt breaks out, and it is only by re-
course to an outburst of primitive fury that the leader

is able to enforce his will. But shortly afterwards the bushes clear and a large expanse of open plain affords them some measure of safety. The men gather round the remains of the wild boar and begin, amidst continual grumbling and mutual threats, to carve the aromatic delicacy in pieces, while the women and children gather a pile of fuel sufficient for the whole night.

The wind has dropped and in the stillness the sensitive ear of the wild man can detect sounds a long distance away. Then suddenly the leader utters that quiet sound, fraught with meaning, that commands the absolute silence and attention of the others. All turn to statues, for in the distance the cry of an animal is again audible and this time louder than before: the jackals have found the first piece of meat and, with unmistakable sounds, two of them are fighting for the plunder. The leader smiles and gives the signal for his companions to continue. A little later, the same growling and snapping of the jaws can be heard, this time still nearer. Again the humans listen attentively. Suddenly the second man jerks round his head and, with a peculiar, tense expression, stares into the face of the leader who, with a satisfied grin, is listening to the fight of the jackals. Now at last, the second man has begun to grasp the leader's intentions. Seizing a few detached ribs, nearly bare of meat, he approaches him, grinning. Then he nudges him and, imitating the barking sound of the jackals, he carries off the bones in the direction from which the band has come. In its tracks, not far from the camp, he stoops to lay them down, then, rising, he looks questioningly at the leader who has been following his actions with interest. They grin at each other and suddenly burst into loud laughter, that same unrestrained mirth that little boys might indulge in to-day when they have succeeded in some particular piece of mischief.

It is already dark and the camp fire is burning as the leader of the band again gives the signal for silence. A gnawing of bones can be heard and, in the light of the fire, the party suddenly see a jackal revelling in the pieces of meat. Once he raises his head, glancing apprehensively towards them, but as nobody attempts to move, he returns again to the feast, and they continue to watch him quietly. In the truest sense, an epoch-making happening: the first time a useful animal has been fed by man! And as at last they lie down to sleep they do so with a feeling of safety which they have not had for a long time.

Many years have passed, many generations. The jackals have become tamer and bolder, and now surround the camps of man in larger packs. Men have now added wild horses and stags to their prey and the jackals too have altered their habits: whereas formerly they remained concealed by day and only ventured abroad by night, now the strongest and cleverest amongst them have become diurnal and follow men on their hunting expeditions. And so some such episode as the following may well have taken place when hunters were following the trail of a pregnant wild mare that has been lamed by a spear wound: they are highly elated, their rations having been meagre for some time now, and the jackals are following them more eagerly than usual since they too have received little or no share of the spoils for an equal period. The mare, weakened by her condition and by loss of blood, resorts to an age-old strategy of her species and lays a false trail, that is,

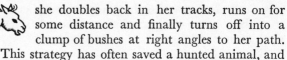

she doubles back in her tracks, runs on for some distance and finally turns off into a clump of bushes at right angles to her path. This strategy has often saved a hunted animal, and on this occasion too the hunters stand baffled at the point where the tracks apparently end.

The jackals follow at a safe distance, still fearing to approach too close to the clamorous hunters. They follow the trail of the humans and not of the wild mare, since, as can be readily understood, they have no desire to overtake on their own an animal which is far too large a prey for them. But these jackals have often been given scraps of large animals whose scents have thus acquired for them a special meaning, and at the same time they have conceived an association of thought between a trail of blood and the near prospect of a feed. To-day the jackals, being particularly hungry, are strongly stimulated by the fresh blood, and now something happens which inaugurates a new form of relationship between man and his band of retainers: the old, grey-muzzled bitch, the potential leader of the pack, notices something which the human hunters have overlooked, namely, the deflection of the trail of blood. The jackals turn off at this point and follow the trail independently, and the hunters, realizing that a false trail has been laid, turn back too. On their arrival at the junction of the paths they hear the jackals howling from one side, and, following the sound, they see the tracks where the many jackals have trodden down the grass of the plain. And here, for the first time, the order is laid down in which man and dog shall pursue their quarry from this day forth: first the dog and then the man. The jackals are swifter than the hunters in overtaking the mare and bringing it to bay.

When a large wild animal is brought to bay by

dogs, a particular psychological mechanism plays
an essential role: the hunted stag, bear or wild boar
which flees from man but does not hesitate to defend
itself against dogs, forgets its more dangerous enemy
in its anger at its impertinent smaller aggressors. The
weary mare, which sees in the jackals only a set of
cowardly yappers, takes up a defensive attitude and
lashes out wildly with one fore-foot at a jackal which
has ventured too close. Now, breathing heavily,
the mare circles but does not resume its flight. In
the meanwhile, the hunters, hearing the sound of the
jackals now concentrated in one spot, soon reach the
scene of action and, at a given signal, distribute themselves silently around their prey. At this, the jackals
move as though to disperse but, seeing that nobody
interferes with them, decide to remain. The leader
of the pack, now devoid of all fear, barks furiously at
the mare, and when it sinks down, impaled by a
spear, buries her teeth ravenously in its throat and
only retreats when the leader of the hunters approaches the carcase. This man, perhaps the great,
great, great grandson of the one who first threw a
piece of meat to the jackals, slits open the belly of
the still twitching mare and tears out a portion of
gut. Without looking directly at the jackals—an act
of intuitive tact—he throws it, not at, but to the
side of the animals—another instance of the same
tact. The grey pack-leader shrinks back a little, then,
seeing that the man makes no threatening gesture,
but only utters a friendly sound, such as the jackals
have often heard from the side of the camp fire, she
falls upon the piece of entrail. As she withdraws,
holding the booty between her fangs and hurriedly
chewing it, she glances back furtively at the man and
at the same time her tail begins to move in little
short strokes from side to side. For the first time a

Huuu- huuiiu - huu

jackal has wagged its tail at a man and thus we get a step nearer to friendship between mankind and the dog. Even such intelligent animals as canine beasts of prey do not acquire an entirely new type of behaviour reaction through a sudden experience, but rather by an association of ideas which is only built up after many recurrences of the same situation. Months probably elapsed before this jackal bitch again ran before the hunter after a big game animal which had laid a false trail, and perhaps it was an even later descendant which regularly and consciously led human beings and brought the game to bay.

At the beginning of the later stone age, man seems to have made his first settlements. The first houses which we know of were situated on pillars and built by the lake dwellers, for reasons of safety, in the shallows of lakes, rivers, and even of the Baltic Sea. We know that at this time the dog had already become domesticated, for the skulls of the little Spitz-like Turf-dogs, which were first found among the remains of the pillar dwellings on the Baltic Sea, though showing plain evidence of their descent from the jackal, also show unmistakable signs of domestication.

The important point is however that, although jackals were at that time more widely distributed than they are to-day, there were no indigenous ones left on the Baltic coasts. In all probability it was man, in his advance further northwards and westwards, who brought with him the dogs or half-tame jackals that followed his camps. When man began to erect his habitations on pillars in the water and invented the canoe, two innovations which certainly meant cultural progress, a basic change in his relations with his four-footed followers must inevitably have followed. Owing to the water these could no longer surround his camps, nor could they guard the

homes of their masters against attacks from human
enemies on the water side. It is reasonable to suppose
that when man first exchanged his camps for pillar
dwellings he brought with him some few tamer specimens of the still half-wild jackals which had particularly distinguished themselves in the chase, and
thus made them into house-dogs in the true sense of
the word. Even to-day different peoples keep dogs
in different ways, the most primitive of these being
when a large number of dogs surrounds a settlement
but only has a very loose connection with man. We
find another type of dog-keeping in every European
country village, where a few dogs belong to a certain
house and are dependent on one particular master.
This last type of relationship very likely evolved with
the development of the pillar dwellings. The smaller
number of dogs which could be accommodated in
the pillar dwellings naturally led to in-breeding
which favoured the hereditary transmission of the
characters of true domestication. Two facts strengthen
these assumptions: first, that the turf-dog, with its
shorter muzzle and somewhat more domed skull, is
certainly a domesticated form of the jackal, and
secondly that the bones of this form have been found
almost exclusively amongst the remains of the settlements of the lake dwellers.

The dogs of the lake dwellers must have been tame
enough either to enter a canoe or to swim the intermediate stretch of water and clamber up the landing-
stage. A half-tame pariah dog would not do this at
any price, and even a young dog of my own stud
requires very patient coaxing before it can be in-
duced to enter my canoe for the first time or to climb
into a tram or railway carriage.

The taming of the dog had possibly already been
achieved when men began to build their pillar

dwellings, or, alternatively, it took place contemporaneously with it. It is quite conceivable that at this time a woman or a little girl 'playing dolls' brought up an orphaned puppy in their family circle. Perhaps the pup was the sole survivor of a litter carried off by a sabre-toothed tiger. The little creature may have cried but probably nobody bothered, for in those days man was insensitive.

But while the men were out hunting and the women fishing, we can well imagine how a little lake-dweller's daughter followed the direction of the whimpering and found at last in some cavity the tiny puppy which wobbled fearlessly towards her and began to lick and suck at her outstretched hands. The soft, round, woolly bundle no doubt elicited in that small daughter of the early stone age the desire to cuddle it and carry it round interminably, just like the little daughters of our own times; for the maternal instincts which give rise to such behaviour are age-old. And so the little stone-age girl, in playful imitation of the actions of the women, gave the puppy food, and her joy at the greed with which it devoured it was no less than that of our women of to-day when a carefully prepared meal gives obvious pleasure to guests. The home-coming parents find with astonishment but little enthusiasm a sleepy little jackal, fat with food. The father, of course, wants to drown it straight away, but his little daughter, weeping, clasps her father's knee so that he stumbles and drops the pup, and when he stoops to pick it up it is already in the arms of the child who is standing in the farthest corner of the room, dissolved in tears. Not even a stone-age father could be so stony-hearted, so the pup is allowed to stay. Thanks to abundant food, he is soon a particularly big, strong animal whose ardent affection for the child now undergoes a

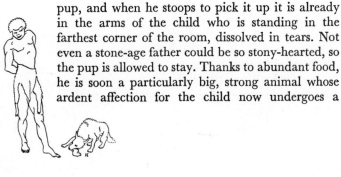

change: although the father, the head of the colony, takes little notice of the dog, it gradually transfers its allegiance from the child to the parent; in fact the time has arrived when the animal, in its wild state, would be breaking away from its mother. Hitherto the daughter has played the role of mother in the life of the puppy, but now the father represents the leader to whom belongs the unswerving pack loyalty of the wild dog. To begin with, the man finds this attachment tiresome, but he soon realizes that this tame dog is much more useful for hunting than the half-wild jackals that hang round the shores of the settlement and, still fearful of man, often make off at the moment when they should be holding a game animal at bay. In its attitude towards the game, the tame dog is also much more courageous than his wild confederates, for his sheltered life in the pillar dwelling has been free from painful experiences with large beasts of prey. So the dog soon becomes the close companion of the man, much to the chagrin of the little daughter, who now only sees her former charge when her father is at home—and stone-age fathers were often absent for long periods. However, in the spring, when jackals bear their young, the father comes home one evening with a skin bag in which there is much heaving and squeaking; and when he opens it—the little daughter jumps for joy—out roll four balls of fur. Only the mother makes an earnest grimace: after all, two would have been enough ...

Did it really happen like this? Well, none of us was there, but considering all we know, it is quite conceivable that it may have done. At the same time, we must not conceal the fact that we do not know for certain that it was exclusively the golden jackal (*Canis aureus*) that attached itself to man in the way described. It is indeed very probable that in different parts of the earth various larger and wolf-like species of jackal became domesticated and later interbred, just as many other forms of domestic animals originate from more than one wild progenitor. A very strong argument in favour of this theory is that pariah dogs do not at all tend to mingle and to re-cross with wild Canis aureus. Mr Shebbeare has very kindly drawn my attention to the fact that there are lots of localities in the near East where Pie dogs and golden jackals abound, yet never intermingle. However, it is quite certain that the northern wolf is not the ancestor of most of our domestic dogs as was formerly believed. There are just a few breeds of dog which are mainly though not entirely, descended from wolves, and these, by their very peculiarities, supply us with the best proof that they are the exception to the rule. These breeds, whose resemblance to the wolf is not merely physical—Eskimo dogs, Samoyeds, Russian Lajkas, Chow-chows, and a few others—all originate from the extreme north. None of them is purely wolf-blooded: it can be assumed with a fair degree of certainty that man, in his advance further and further north, brought with him some already domesticated, jackal-blooded dogs, from which, after repeated crossings with wolf-blooded animals, these breeds arose. I shall have a lot more to say about the peculiar mental propensities of wolf-blooded dogs.

In contrast to the dog, the cat has only become domesticated in recent times, that is to say, as far as it has ever become domesticated at all. By recent I mean relatively to the dog, which, according to people who should know, dates back between forty and sixty thousand years. I should reckon that the first

feeding of a jackal by a man took place about
50,000 years ago, and the first adoption of a dog in
a pillar dwelling about 20,000 years before historic
times. As opposed to these, the alliance of the cat
with man derives, in a manner of speaking, from
yesterday. The same people that in the next millen-
ium were to build the pyramid of Cheops were
already building up a higher form of culture: cattle,
sheep and horses were domestic animals just as we
know them to-day, man lived in stone houses and
tilled his fields, and the ox drew the plough—all not
so very different from things in our own times. It was
very probably in Egypt, the first large agrarian land,
that the cat attached itself to man; in Egypt, whose
great corn chambers are already mentioned in the
Bible. Where there are large granaries mice and rats
are always to be found in large numbers, and if mice
had no place in the seven plagues of Egypt described
in the Old Testament, it is surely because they were
an ever-present plague and an increase in their
numbers could have made very little impression.
That the ancient Egyptians were fine observers of
nature is evident from the wonderful animal studies
in their frescoes, and there is no doubt that they knew
exactly which of their indigenous small predatory
beasts were inimical to mice and rats. The Ichneu-
mon, also called Pharaoh's rat, was a native of
Egypt, described by Herodotus as a sacred animal,
and the cat (*Felis ocreata*), an inhabitant of Africa and
Syria and the wild ancestor of our domestic cat, is
to be found carefully embalmed in the tombs of the
middle Egyptian kingdom. However, research into
the history of the domestic cat has revealed that the
cat was not revered for its own sake, but as a symbol
of the lioness which in ancient Egypt, was sacred to
the goddess Basd. One can scarcely blame the priests

of that goddess for choosing for their ceremonies a smaller and more tractable animal than a lioness, however tame the latter happened to be. Probably such an animal had once made itself unpopular by eating a portly Basd priest on a ceremonial occasion. But joking apart, the cat as a symbol of the lion, as a miniature edition of the royal beast of prey, is a thought which much appeals to me; for me, too, the charm of the cat lies in the fact that she displays to me, within the confines of my own home, the unbroken wildness and the subtle grace which she shares with the panther, the jaguar, and the tiger, and possesses in no less measure than they. Anyone who has had the opportunity of knowing an African wild cat more intimately will have no doubt that no great effort would be needed to make a creature of this species into a domestic animal. In a way it is a born domestic animal. While captive adult specimens of the European wild cat (*Felis silvestris*) are completely untameable and even those caught young remain permanently wild and intractable, even adult African wild cats become tame so quickly, without any particular effort on the part of their keepers, that after quite a short time a cage seems an unnecessary cruelty. In many a zoological garden, a cat which has arrived as a captive has later become a favourite of its keeper and 'taken on the job' of house cat. Among my many animal acquaintances, I can think of no really wild or shy African cat or any really tame European wild cat. When the ancient Egyptians, wisely appreciating its importance, put the cat under legislative protection —it is a historical fact that they imposed the death penalty for the killing of one of these animals—it was inevitable that the sacred cats should lose all fear of man in the course of a few generations and became

just as obtrusively tame as the sacred cows of the
Hindus are to-day; and if these humped cattle are so
sure of their invulnerability as to invade the street
stalls and, to the horror of the powerless stallholders,
to devour their most succulent fruit and vegetables,
how much quicker must the far cleverer sacred cats
have been to see their advantage and to make use of
the proverbial flesh pots of Egypt; though it is to be
hoped that they did not neglect their duties as
mouse-catchers at the same time.

We can imagine how superciliously a cat of those
times must have treated its host when even our common cats of to-day rarely give their masters much
attention; indeed the latter may feel genuinely flattered if the little tigers offer them from time to time a
few gestures of politeness or affection. There is a connection between the independence of the cat and the
slow rate at which the physical signs of its domestication have made their appearance. Although the cat
was proclaimed a sacred temple animal in about the
fifth or sixth dynasty, it is only in feline mummies of
the twelfth and thirteenth dynasties that the slightest
signs of the mutations of domesticity have been
found, such as appreciable alterations in the structure of the ear, and changes of colour, which already
at that time showed the most various shades, although
black, white and mottled were not yet amongst
them. It was also at that time that the skull of the
cat began to show doming of the temporal parts and
shortening of the nasal regions, features which had
already typified the turf-dog as a domestic animal
some tens of thousands of years earlier. Even to-day,
in cats which have not been bred to a very particular
ideal, the physical and mental mutations of domesticity have made little progress, and thin, long-
legged, short-haired cats with tiger markings, such

as are not seldom found in Central Europe, bear an amazing resemblance to Falbkatze cats.

Although the cat was widely distributed as a domestic animal in Egypt since early times, it took an incredibly long time to penetrate to other lands. Most of the writers on ancient Europe knew next to nothing about it, and it is Plutarch who first tells us, in the first century A.D., of the advent of the cat to Europe. Curiously, enough together with it he mentions the weasel as a useful animal kept exclusively for the destruction of mice. At that time the weasel had evidently not yet been supplanted by the much more easily kept household cat. The further distribution of the domestic cat throughout Europe proceeded extraordinarily slowly: in the laws of Howell Dhu of Wales, there are definite regulations as to the price that may be asked for a cat and what qualities the buyer has the right to demand. At that time, about A.D. 1000, anybody who killed a cat had to expiate his crime with a sheep, or a lamb, or with as much wheat as would completely cover the dead cat suspended at full length over the ground by its tail. As a corpse becomes considerably elongated by such treatment, quite a large amount of wheat must have been required.

In the 8th century there were apparently no cats in Germany, or at least there is no mention of them in the Salic laws. Here in the 14th century, the cat seems still to have been extremely valuable, for, in certain contracts of sale, it was counted among the chattels which must be handed over when a farm was disposed of. I have repeated these statements which, admittedly, I have taken from Brehm, for a particular reason: a species of domestic animal, purposely bred by man, and packed in cases for transport, spreads much more quickly than the cat has done. Even to-day, it is not so easy to sell and dispatch a cat, particularly if it possesses that independent hunting spirit which enhances its value as a destroyer of vermin. Led by their still amazingly well preserved sense of direction, cats will return to their old homes over incredible distances and, even if they are sent so far that this is impossible, it does not necessarily follow that they will remain in their new quarters; they may instead take up their independence and return to the wilds. I therefore consider it possible that the cat was not originally spread passively by human beings who traded with it but that, moving from house to house, from village to village, it gradually took possession of the whole continent.

2. TWO ORIGINS OF FIDELITY

EVERYBODY who has owned more than one dog knows how widely individual canine person-alities differ from each other. No two are really alike any more than human beings are, even twins; but even in human beings it is possible to pick out individual traits and, by combining them, to explain up to a certain extent the different temperaments, though character analysis can never attain the grade of an exact natural science, owing to the infinite complexity of its subject. The dog's personality is vastly simpler, and it is much easier to explain the peculiarities of different characters by considering the development of certain 'characteristic' traits, and their combinations in the individual. A thorough, scientific character analysis of the dog would un-doubtedly be beneficial to comparative psychology, since, working on this much simpler model, methods could be devised for the analysis of the most inscrut-able and complicated of all subjects—man.

I do not of course intend, in this book, to attempt a scientific characterology of the domestic dog, but I will try to show how the interaction of some few innate predispositions, in particular of two special ones, produces an extremely finely graded scale of apparently basically different canine characters. These particular properties of the dog are also those

which decide in the first place his relations with his
master and are therefore of great interest to the dog-
lover. The dependence of a dog on his master has
two quite distinct origins; it is largely due to a lifelong maintenance of those ties which bind the young
wild dog to its mother, but which in the domestic
dog remain part of a lifelong preservation of youthful characters. The other root of fidelity arises from
the pack loyalty which binds the wild dog to the
pack-leader or, respectively from the affection which
the individual members of the pack feel for each
other. This root goes much deeper in dogs with more
wolf than jackal blood, for the obvious reason that
the preservation of the pack plays a far larger role in
the life of the wolf. If one takes a young, non-
domesticated canine animal into one's house and
brings it up exactly as a dog, one can easily convince
oneself that the youthful dependence of the wild
animal is identical with those lifelong social ties
which bind most of our domestic dogs to their
masters. Such a young wolf inclines to shyness, pre-
ferring dark corners, and has obvious inhibitions
about crossing open spaces. He is exceedingly mistrustful of strangers and tends to snap savagely and
without warning if a stranger attempts to stroke him.
He is, from birth, in marked measure what we call
an 'Angstbeisser' (a biter from fear), but towards
his master he is just as affectionate and dependent
as a young dog. In the case of a female which, in the
normal course of events, would later accept a male
leader-wolf as her 'boss', an expert trainer may
succeed in taking the place of this leader, at the stage
when the youthful dependence of the female is
diminishing, and thus secure her permanent affection. A Viennese police inspector did actually succeed
in doing this with his well-known wolf bitch, 'Poldi'.

But in the case of a male wolf, the trainer will inevitably be disappointed: as soon as he is fully grown, the animal suddenly swerves from his obedience to his master and becomes independent. He does not become ferocious towards his former master, for he still treats him as a friend, but he no longer dreams of following him blindly and may even make serious attempts to subordinate him and to promote himself to the rank of leader. Owing to the power of the wolf's teeth, this procedure sometimes takes a rather sanguinary course.

The same thing happened with a Dingo which I had acquired on the fifth day of its life, gave to my own bitch to suckle, and on whose education I expended a deal of time and trouble. This wild dog did not attempt to subjugate or to bite me but, when he reached maturity he began to lose his early obedience to me in the most curious fashion. As a young animal his behaviour differed in no way from that of an ordinary dog: when he had been punished for some ill-doing, he showed his bad conscience in the usual way of dogs, that is, he tried to conciliate his angry master by submissive or pleading gestures, nor would he rest until he had obtained the forgiving caress. However, his manner changed entirely when he was about one and a half years old: he still accepted every form of punishment, even a beating, without resistance, but, as soon as the business was over, he shook himself, gave me a friendly wag of his tail and ran off, inviting me to chase him. In other words, his frame of mind was in no way altered by the punishment nor did it have the least influence upon him or hinder him from immediately repeating the crime for which he had just been punished, as, for example, making a renewed attempt to murder one of my most valuable ducks. At the same age he lost all inclination

to accompany me on my walks and simply ran off
anywhere without paying the slightest attention to
my calls. Nevertheless I must stress that he was extremely friendly towards me and greeted me, whenever we happened to meet, with all the usual canine
ceremonial. One must never expect a wild animal
to treat a human being differently from a member
of its own species, and we shall return to this subject
when dealing with the relations between cats and
humans. My Dingo evidently harboured the warmest
feelings for me that such an animal, when mature,
can ever feel for another one, but submission and
obedience play no part in these feelings.

All the higher domesticated dogs, in which jackal
blood is predominant, remain all their lives as dependent on their masters as young wild dogs are on
older animals of their own species; but this is not
the only youthful characteristic which, in contrast to
the wild dog, they retain all their lives: the short
hair, curly tail and hanging ears of many breeds,
above all the shortening of the muzzle and doming
of the skull which we have already seen in the Turf-
dog (*Canis familiaris palustris*) are points that characterize only the young animal in the wild forms, but
which continue at all ages in the domestic dog.

Like most character traits, childishness can be a
merit or a defect according to its extent. Dogs that
are completely lacking in it may be psychologically
interesting in their independence, but will not bring
their masters much pleasure, since they are in-
corrigible vagabonds who only occasionally honour
the house of their owners—one cannot speak of
'masters' in their case—with their presence. As they
become older such dogs are likely to become
dangerous, since, lacking a typical canine submission,
they 'think nothing' of biting and shaking a man

as they would another dog. While condemning this vagabondage and its concomitant lack of fidelity to a master or a place, I must add that an exaggerated persistency of youthful dependence may have consequences surprisingly similar to those following its complete absence. Although a certain degree of persisting youthfulness is, in most of our domestic dogs, the origin of their fidelity, a surfeit of it may lead to exactly the opposite results. Such dogs are then extremely affectionate towards their masters but also towards everyone else. In *King Solomon's Ring* I have already compared this type of dog with those spoilt children who call every man 'Uncle', and importune every stranger with their promiscuous friendliness. It is not that such a dog does not know his master, on the contrary, he welcomes him delightedly and greets him more effusively than he does a stranger, but immediately afterwards he is prepared to run off with the next person who crosses his path. That this indiscriminate friendliness for all mankind is a result of exaggerated infantility is proved by the whole behaviour of dogs of this kind: they are always over-playful, and long after their first year of life, when normal dogs have sobered down, they persist in chewing their master's shoes or shaking the curtains to death; above all, they retain a slave-like submission which in other dogs is supplanted after a few months by a healthy self-confidence. Before every stranger, after they have perhaps dutifully barked at him, they will fall obsequiously on to their backs the moment he speaks sternly to them, and anybody who holds the other end of their lead in his hand is accepted as an awe-inspiring master.

The happy medium between the all-too-dependent and the all-too-independent animal is the ideal character of the really faithful dog. He is much rarer

than is generally supposed, certainly much rarer than
the average dog owner fondly imagines.

A certain degree of retained youthfulness is necessary in order to make a dog attached and faithful to his master, but a little more of the same propensity will make him treat all mankind with the same submissive respect. Thus there are relatively few dogs that will really defend their masters against an aggressor, not because they are left cold by the attack but because any human being is so much an object of respect as to make it well-nigh impossible for them to assault him. My little French bulldog would rush with angry growls at anybody, even a member of the family, who dared to raise his hand to me whether in anger or in fun, and he would seize and shake furiously the skirt or trousers of the offender, but always meticulously avoided including the skin in his bite. My Alsatian, Tito, also, who would bite even my opponent in discussion, never really hurt anybody, even the tramps who came begging to our yard, and her incomparably fiercer grandchild, Stasi, who once threw a general on to his back during the last war and kept him in this comfortable position for a good quarter of an hour, never seriously bit anybody in her life. I do not know how these two bitches would have behaved in the case of a genuine attack on my person but, being far more perceptive than the French bulldog, they never let themselves be roused by a mock assault but merely turned away with an offended glance at myself. I am therefore inclined to think that they would have equally recognized a serious attack and taken measures accordingly.

The fidelity of those breeds in whose veins more or less wolf's blood flows is of a very different kind from that of our Central European breeds which are

probably mainly descended from jackals. I very much
doubt whether there are any dog breeds which are
directly descended from the wolf and I have good
reason for believing that man was already accompanied by jackal dogs when he began to extend his
settlements to the Arctic Circle where he came in
contact with the Arctic wolf. The crossing of wolves
with the domestic dogs of jackal extraction owned by
the Nordic peoples evidently took place relatively
late, certainly much later than the first domestication
of the jackal. Since the wolf is stronger and more
hardy, it was evidently found desirable to introduce
as much wolf blood as possible into the strain, the
resulting specimens probably causing little trouble to
the male dwellers of the Arctic Zones who are born
animal tamers and adept in handling intractable
dogs. As the immediate result of this strong and
relatively recent admixture of wolf blood, the marks
of domesticity particularly that of the persistent
youthfulness are much less distinct in Lupus-blooded
dogs than in those of our Central European breeds.
The place of this trait is taken by a completely different type of dependency which derives its origin from
the specific propensities of the wolf. While the jackal
is chiefly a carrion feeder, the wolf is almost purely a
beast of prey and is dependent on the support of his
fellows in the killing of the large animals which are
his sole means of sustenance in the cold season.

In order to obtain enough nourishment for its
large requirements, the wolf pack is obliged to cover
great distances, when the members must support
each other staunchly in their attacks on big game.
An exacting social organization, true loyalty to the
pack-leader and the absolute mutual support of all
its members are the conditions for success in the
hard struggle for existence of this species. These

properties of the wolf explain without any doubt the very noticeable difference in disposition between jackal and Lupus dogs, which is quite apparent to people with a real understanding of dogs. While the former treat their masters as parent animals, the latter see them more in the light of pack-leaders and their behaviour towards them is correspondingly different.

The submissiveness of the childish jackal dog is matched in the Lupus dog by a proud 'man to man' loyalty which includes little submission and less obedience. On the other hand, the allegiance of the Lupus dog to his master is a much stronger one than that of the jackal dog. The Lupus dog does not possess those Oedipus complexes of the more domesticated dog which convert his master to a cross between a father and a god; he treats him much more as a colleague, although his bond with him is very much stronger and far less transferable to another person. This unique attachment to a certain person develops in young Lupus dogs in a peculiar way: there is a definite transition from the child-like dependence on the parent to an adult allegiance to a pack-leader, and this takes place even when the young dog grows up without contacts with his own kind and when 'parent animal' and 'pack-leader' are represented by one and the same human being. The phenomenon resembles that of the young man, who at the time of puberty, separates himself from his family with all its traditions and embraces new ideals; and let the youth beware who, at this most impressionable period, hangs his heart on a false idol!

3. CANINE PERSONALITIES

IN this chapter, I shall try to illustrate by a few concrete examples, how the character traits mentioned in the previous pages can influence the personalities of individual dogs. In doing so, I shall deal rather broadly with the two contrasting groups of dogs which show in their temperaments either the absolute persistence of youthful dependency, or its complete absence combined with the corresponding degree of loyalty to a pack-leader which is usually associated with these features.

I shall begin with the example of a dog whose apparently touching juvenile affection was so exaggerated as to result in a positive caricature of a dog. It was a dachshund called Kroki which I was given by a kind relation with no understanding of animals. At the time I was a small boy but already an active naturalist. The dog was called Kroki because the kind donor had first of all presented me with a crocodile which, in the absence of adequate heating in my terrarium, refused to eat and which we therefore exchanged in the pet shop for the animal which bore the nearest outward resemblance to it! This dachshund was an aristocratic creature, long-bodied and short-legged—truly resembling a crocodile—and its pendulous ears literally trailed the floor. He was of an affecting friendliness and greeted me on our first acquaintance as only a dog can greet a long lost master. Of course I was flattered, until it became clear to me that he greeted everybody else in the same manner. He was obsessed by an overwhelming love of humanity which extended to all mankind. He never barked at anybody and, even though he probably preferred my family and myself, he would readily follow a stranger if we did not happen to be available. He did not improve as he grew older and we were continually obliged to fetch him home from the various houses where he paid visits. Finally, my cousin, who had a soft spot for the handsome dog, took him to live with her in Grinzing, where he continued his promiscuous mode of life in this bacchanalian suburb of Vienna. He lived with all sorts of different families for quite irregular periods of time, and several times he was stolen and sold to unwitting people who were charmed by his 'devotion'. Possibly it was always the same thief who, acquainted with the dog's habits, stole him from time to time and made a small living out of him.

The diametrical opposite of this dachshund is Wolf, one of our two present house-dogs, if he can be described as such. He is the typical, non-infantile, completely independent Lupus dog, subject to nobody; in fact he considers himself as the leader of our 'pack'. His character derives from his own peculiar history.

The impressionable period at which a Lupus dog attaches itself for better or worse to one human being is generally relatively early in its life, round about the fifth month. I once paid dearly for my ignorance of this fact: our first Chow bitch was acquired as a birthday present for my wife and, intending it to be a surprise, I asked my cousin to keep the pup—

which was just under six months old—for the week before the occasion. Believe it or not, those seven days sufficed for the little dog to fix its affection immutably on my cousin, a state of affairs which rather detracted from the value of the birthday present. Although my cousin rarely came to see us, the temperamental little Chow quite clearly regarded her, and not my wife, as her rightful owner. Admittedly, she gradually became fond of my wife but she would undoubtedly have been much more so if I had brought her straight home from the breeding kennel. Even after years, she would have been ready to leave us for her first 'owner'.

This period in which a master is chosen by such a dog may pass by unheeded, perhaps because the dog has lived for too long in kennels or because for some other reason, it has had no chance of finding a suitable master. In both cases, a peculiar and extraordinarily independent canine character evolves, which is personified in Wolf. He was born just after the second World War, when food was very scarce, and my wife kept him as a present for me on my imminently expected return. Unfortunately, my return was delayed indefinitely and the dog had nobody to attach himself to during this impressionable period. His litter sister lived and still lives with a publican in the next village, who is a passionate dog-lover and a successful breeder of Chows. It did not take Wolf long to seek out his sister in her luxurious new home and, at the age of about seven months, to move in there himself. At the same time, by means of the supercilious charm which distinguishes him, he had wormed his way into at least two other houses of the neighbourhood, and, at one period, there were four families which flattered themselves that they owned the handsome dog. In this way he had reached the age of eighteen months when, in 1948, I finally returned home from Russia where I had been held prisoner of war. Tactfully and unobtrusively, I managed to gain his confidence in so far that he would voluntarily accompany me on long walks although, admittedly, I could never guarantee that he would not suddenly desert me for some other interest. The only way I could keep him close to me was by encouraging him to follow my bicycle for increasingly long distances. In entirely strange regions, far beyond the bounds of a dog's own independent excursions, where a human friend is the only familiar object, the relation of the dog to his master is similar to that of the wolf to the experienced pack-leader which conducts him across unknown territory. In this way, the man acquires, for the dog, the status of leader-wolf, and I know of no better way of bringing a dog to accept one as his master. He keeps in ever closer contact with him, the more unfamiliar the surroundings become; thus a neighbourhood in which the animal feels bewildered is particularly effective: take a country-reared dog to town, where the many disturbing stimuli of trams, cars, strange smells and people upset his self confidence, making him afraid to lose his one friend, and the most disobedient animal will walk to heel like a well-trained police-dog. Of course, one must avoid taking him into a too fear-inspiring region, otherwise, though he will stick to his master exemplarily on the first occasion, he will simply refuse to accompany him a second time, and an attempt to drag a strong charactered dog forcibly on the lead would have exactly the opposite effect to the one desired.

I succeeded in commanding Wolf's respect in so far that he moved his quarters from the public house back to ours, and he acknowledged me as master to the extent that he would accompany me everywhere even to places uncongenial to him. But that was as far as it went. Of obedience he showed not a vestige, and even now he is often missing for days at a time. Until just lately, he was always absent on Saturdays and Sundays. This first came to my notice when I found the dog was never there at week-ends when I wished to show him to our visitors. The solution to the riddle was that he spent every Saturday afternoon and the whole of Sunday ... in the pub! He had evidently found out that the 'tit-bits' in this hospitable house were particularly abundant and the presence of two handsome Chow ladies may also have helped to make him feel at home there.

The loose bonds of friendship which unite me with Wolf provide me with an inexhaustible fund of instruction and amusement. It is extraordinarily interesting for an animal psychologist to study a dog which bears no allegiance and has no sense of obedience to any human being; Wolf was the first dog of this kind I ever got to know well. And it is extremely funny how everybody—myself included—who knows this proud, imperious dog, feels flattered if he honours them with a majestic indication of his favour. Even Susi shows a respectful admiration for him which often makes me quite jealous.

After these descriptions of the dachshund Kroki, and the Chow, Wolf, who, for diametrically opposed reasons, found no contact with a master, I shall depict, as a third canine personality, the character of my bitch, Stasi. In her relationship to her master were combined happily the strong, youthful dependence of her great grandmother, Tito, and an exclusive loyalty to the pack-leader, inherited from her Lupus-blooded ancestors.

Stasi was born in our house in early spring, 1940,

and was seven months old when I adopted her as my own and began to train her. In her outward appearance, as in her temperament, the characters of the Alsatian and the Chow were mixed in a particularly favourable way. With her sharp, wolf-like muzzle, wide cheek-bones, slanting eyes and short, hairy ears, with her short, bushy tail and, above all, her wonderfully elastic and elegant movements, she resembled more than anything else a little female wolf; only the flaming golden-red of her coat betrayed very literally her Aureus blood. But the true gold was in her character. She learned the rudiments of canine education, walking on the lead, walking to heel, and 'lying down', astonishingly quickly. She was more or less spontaneously house-clean and safe with poultry, so that there was no need to teach her those attributes.

After two short months, my bond with this dog was broken by the force of destiny: I was called to the University of Königsberg as professor of psychology and I left my family, home and dogs on September 2nd, 1940. When I returned at Christmas for a short holiday, Stasi greeted me in a frenzy of joy, demonstrating that her great love for me was unchanged. She could do everything I had taught her, just as well as before, and was indeed exactly the same dog as I had left behind me four months previously. But tragic scenes were enacted when I began to prepare for my departure. Many dog-lovers will know what I mean. Even before the suit-case packing—the visible sign of departure—had started, the dog became noticeably depressed and refused to leave my side for an instant. With nervous haste, she sprang up and followed every time I left the room, even accompanying me to the bathroom. When the trunks were packed and my departure became imminent, the misery of poor Stasi waxed to the point of desperation, almost to a neurosis. She would not eat and her breathing became abnormal, very shallow and punctuated now and then by great, deep sighs. Before I left, we decided to shut her up, to prevent her making a violent attempt to follow me. But now, strangely, the little bitch, who had not left my side for days, retired to the garden and would not come when I called her. The most obedient of all dogs had become refractory, and all our efforts to catch her were in vain. When, finally, with the usual retinue of children, a hand-cart and luggage, I started out for the station, a strange looking dog, with lowered tail, ruffled mane and wild eyes, followed us at a distance of twenty-five yards. At the station, I made a last attempt to catch her, but it was hopeless. Even when I boarded the train, she still stood in the defiant attitude of a rebellious dog, with lowered ears and ruffled mane, watching me suspiciously from a safe distance. The train began to pull out of the station, and still the dog stood rooted to the spot. But as the engine increased its speed, she suddenly shot forward, rushing alongside the train, and leaping up into it, three carriages in front of the one on whose platform I was still standing in order to prevent her jumping on to it. (On the Austrian local trains, there is a fairly spacious platform at each end of and communicating with the carriages.) I ran forward, seized her by the skin of her neck and rump and thrust her from the train, which was already moving quite fast. She landed dexterously on her feet, without falling. No longer in defiant attitude, but with ears pricked and head on one side, she watched the train until it was out of sight.

In Königsberg, I soon received disturbing news of Stasi: she had killed a whole series of our neighbour's

hens, had started roaming restlessly about the district, was no longer house-trained and refused to obey anybody. Her only use now was as a watch-dog, for she was becoming increasingly ferocious. After she had committed a long list of crimes—several hen murders, the burglary of a rabbit hutch, with much ensuing bloodshed, and finally the tearing of the postman's trousers, she was degraded to the status of a yard-dog and sat in sorrowful solitude on the terrace adjoining the west side of our house. In actual fact, she was only solitary in regard to human company, for she shared a large and elegant kennel with the handsome Dingo dog of which I have already told in the first chapter of this book. From shortly after Christmas till July, she was caged like a wild animal in the company of a wild animal.

On my return to Altenberg at the end of June, 1940, I went straight into the garden to see Stasi. As I climbed the steps to the terrace, both dogs rushed at me furiously, as furiously as only dogs deprived of their freedom can. I stood still on the top step and the dogs came nearer, barking and growling angrily, for the direction of the wind was such that they could not pick up my scent. I wondered when they would recognize me visually, but they did not do this at all. Quite suddenly, Stasi scented me and what now took place I shall never forget: in the midst of a heated onrush, she stopped abruptly and stiffened to a statue. Her mane was still ruffled, her tail down and her ears flat, but her nostrils were wide, wide open, inhaling greedily the message carried by the wind. Now the raised crest subsided, a shiver ran through her body and she pricked up her ears. I expected her to throw herself at me in a burst of joy, but she did not. The mental suffering which

had been so severe as to alter the dog's whole personality, causing this most tractable of creatures to forget manners, law and order for months, could not
fade into nothingness in a second. Her hind legs gave
way, her nose was directed skywards, something
happened in her throat, and then the mental torture
of months found outlet in the hair-raising yet beautiful tones of a wolf's howl. For a long time, perhaps
for half a minute, she howled, then, like a thunderbolt, she was upon me. I was enveloped in a whirl-
wind of ecstatic canine joy, she leapt to my shoulders,
nearly tearing the clothes from my back, she—the
exclusive, undemonstrative, whose greeting normally
consisted of a few restrained tail-wags, the highest
sign of whose affection was a head laid upon my
knee, she, the silent one, whistled in her excitement
like a locomotive, and cried in piercing tones, even
louder than her howls of a few seconds before. Then
she suddenly desisted, ran past me towards the gate,
where she stopped, looking round at me over her
shoulder and begging to be let out. It was self-evident
to her that, with my return, her imprisonment was
also at an end, and she returned quite simply to the
order of the day. Lucky animal, enviable robustness
of the nervous system! A mental trauma whose cause
is removed leaves in animals no after-effects which
cannot be healed by a howl of thirty seconds' duration and a dance for joy of a minute and a half,
healed so completely that the animal can return at
once to normal.

As I went back to the house with Stasi at my side,
my wife, who saw us coming, cried 'Good heavens,
the hens!' Stasi did not so much as look at a single
hen. In the evening, when I brought her into the
house, my wife warned me that the dog was no longer
'clean'. Stasi was as perfectly house-trained as she

had ever been. She could still do everything I had ever taught her and was still the same dog which my scarcely two months of training had made her. During nine months of the deepest sorrow which can ever befall a dog, she had faithfully conserved all that she owed to me. And now followed for Stasi weeks of the purest delight. During that summer vacation, she was my inseparable companion, and nearly every day we took long walks beside the Danube, often swimming in the river. But even the best holidays come to an end, and when the time came to pack the suit-cases, the tragedy that I have already described threatened to repeat itself. Stasi was still and despondent and kept close to my side. This time, the undeniable fact that a dog does not understand human words as such, cost the poor animal days of misery. I had decided to take her with me, but I could not tell her so; though I constantly assured her that I would not leave her behind, her state of nervous tension was maintained and she would not let me out of her sight. But, in the end, I did make her understand: shortly before my departure, the bitch again retired to the garden, evidently with the same intentions as before. I left her alone until I was ready to start, when I summoned her in the same tone of voice which I used when calling her for a walk. Then she suddenly understood and danced round me in a veritable orgy of relief.

Stasi was only able to remain with her master for a few months for on October 10th, 1941, I was called up for military service. The same parting tragedy took place, with the only difference that, this time, Stasi ran away, made herself entirely independent and, for two months, led the life of a wild animal in the precincts of Königsberg perpetrating crime upon crime. I have no doubt whatever that she was the mysterious 'fox' which plundered the rabbit hutches of a councillor in the Caecilean Allee. After Christmas, terribly thin and discharging from eyes and nose, Stasi returned home to my wife who nursed her back to health. But it was impossible to keep her at home, so she was sent to live at the Königsberg Zoo, where she shared the cage of the great Siberian wolf who became her husband. Unfortunately the marriage was childless. Months later when I was working as neurologist in the military hospital at Posen, I took Stasi to live with me again. In June, 1944, I was sent to the front, and Stasi and her six children went to the Schönbrunn Zoo at Vienna, where, towards the end of the war, she was killed in an air-raid. But one of our neighbours in Altenberg had acquired her son from whom all our present dogs are descended. Stasi spent rather less than half her six years of life in the company of her master, but nevertheless, she was the most faithful dog that I have ever known ... and I have known a great many dogs.

4. TRAINING

THERE are already many excellent books on the training of dogs, written by people better qualified than I am, and I am not going to make this chapter a treatise on canine education. I only wish to discuss a few easily attained feats of training which should simplify any dog owner's relations with his charge. The average modern dog owner probably derives little or no advantage from the animal which is trained to attack "a thief" on command, to retrieve heavy objects or to find lost ones, and I ask the lucky master of such a clever dog, how often within the last years has his companion had the opportunity of putting all these arts into practice? I myself have never yet been saved by a dog from a burglar and the only time that a dog of mine ever brought me an object lost on the street, it happened to be a bitch that had never been trained to retrieve. It was quite a remarkable experience: Pygi II, daughter of the already often mentioned Stasi, who was trotting after me in the streets of Königsberg, suddenly nudged me in the leg with her nose and, as I glanced down at her, she raised her jaws which clasped a lost leather glove. What she was thinking at the time, and whether she really had the ghost of an idea that the object lying in my wake and infused with my smell really belonged to me, I do not know. Of course, after that, I repeatedly 'lost' gloves but never, never again did she so much as look at them. However, I wonder how many dogs which are perfectly trained to 'seek lost' have ever brought back to their masters genuinely lost articles.

In *King Solomon's Ring*, I have already expressed my opinion, in no uncertain terms, on the subject of giving one's dog to a professional trainer for its up-bringing. The three lessons which I am going to discuss here are, in themselves, quite elementary, and yet it is surprising how few dog owners will take the trouble to teach them to their dogs: namely, 'Lie down', 'Basket' and 'Heel'.

But first of all, a few general remarks on the rules of dog training. To begin with, the question of reward and punishment; it is a fundamental error to consider the latter more efficacious than the former. Many branches of canine education particularly 'house-training', are much better instilled without the aid of punishment. The best way to 'house-train' a newly acquired young dog of about three months is to watch him constantly during his first few hours in your house and to interrupt him the moment he seems likely to deposit a *corpus delicti* of either liquid or solid consistency. Carry him as quickly as possible outside and set him down,  always in the same place. When he has done what is required of him praise and caress him as though he had performed a positive act of heroism. A puppy treated like this very soon learns what is meant, and if he is taken out regularly, there will soon be nothing more to clean up.

The most important thing is that punishment should follow an offence as quickly as possible. There is no sense in beating a dog even a few minutes after he has done something wrong, since he cannot understand the connection. Only in the case of habitual

offenders which are quite conscious of their mis-
doings is delayed punishment likely to be of any use.
There are, of course, exceptions to this rule: on the
occasions when a dog of mine has killed a new animal
of my collection simply out of ignorance, I have been
able to impress upon him the enormity of his conduct
by hitting him later with the corpse. This was not so
much calculated to imbue the dog with the wrong-
ness of a certain deed as to fill him with revulsion for
a certain object. As I shall describe later I have
resorted in certain cases to 'prophylactic punishment' in order to inculcate in the dogs a feeling for
the sanctity of new house-mates.

It is quite wrong to attempt to instil obedience
into a dog by punishment, and equally senseless to
beat him afterwards when, enticed by the scent of
some game, he has run away during a walk. The
beating will cure him, not of running away, which
lies further back in his memory, but probably of the
coming back, with which he will assuredly connect
the punishment. The only way of curing such a de-
serter is to shoot something at him with a catapult
just as he is preparing to make off. The shot must
take the dog quite by surprise and it is better that
he should not notice that this bolt from the blue was
directed by the hand of his own master. The complete defencelessness of the animal against this sudden
pain will make it all the more memorable for him,
and this method has the additional advantage that
it will not make him 'hand-shy'.

Where corporal punishment is concerned the same
principles apply both for dogs and children: it should
be administered only by a person who is really fond
of the culprit and who thereby hurts himself almost
more than he does the offender, and much fine feeling and understanding of dogs is required in the

gradation of the sentence. Sensitivity to punishment varies considerably in different dogs and a light slap may mean more to a highly-strung, impressionable dog than a severe beating to his more robust brother. Physically, a healthy dog is an extraordinarily insensitive creature and, apart from striking him on the nose, it is almost impossible to hurt him with the bare hand. My Alsatian, Tito, was a physically very robust dog and often knocked me black and blue when playing. On such occasions I could deal out blows to her with my fists and feet or fling her roughly to the ground as she hung on to my arm and she regarded the rough treatment as a grand sport which gave her the opportunity for still rougher reprisals. On the other hand, if I really meant it seriously, the slightest tap was enough to make her yelp and shrink into herself unhappily.

When in the same dog mental and physical sensitiveness are combined, as often happens in the case of spaniels, setters and other similar breeds, much care must be taken in meting out corporal chastisement, otherwise the dog may easily become intimidated, lose its self-confidence and *joie de vivre*, finally even becoming permanently hand-shy. During my experiments in cross-breeding Chows with Alsatians, particularly at the beginning when the stud contained rather more Alsatian blood, extremes of temperament from very 'soft' and impressionable to completely insensitive ones were often to be found quite irregularly distributed amongst these dogs.

Stasi was an extraordinarily 'tough' dog, while her daughter, Pygi, was the exact opposite. On occasions when the two had again diverged from the straight and narrow path (as when they nearly pulled a Maltese terrier in half) passers-by were in-dignant at my apparent injustice, for I invariably flogged the mother and let the daughter go with a light slap and an angry remonstrance. Nevertheless, both dogs had received an equivalent punishment. Every form of canine punishment is effective less by virtue of the pain it causes than by revelation of the power of the administrator. It is most essential for the efficacy of the punishment that the dog really understands this revelation of power. Since dogs, like monkeys, do not hit but bite each other in their ranking order disputes, the blow is not really an adequate or intelligible form of chastisement. My friend, the late Count Max Thun-Hohenstein, found that a nip in the arm or shoulder, which did not even produce a wound, made on a monkey an incomparably deeper impression than the most severe beating. But of course biting monkeys is not to everybody's taste. In dogs, though, one can imitate the penal methods of a pack-leader and involve one's own personal feelings much less by lifting the dog up by the neck and shaking him. This is the severest way that I know of punishing a dog and it never fails to make a deep impression on the offender. In actual fact, a wolf-leader which could lift up a dog of Alsatian size and shake it would be a giant, a super-wolf, and as such the dog regards his master in the moment of chastisement. Although this form of punishment seems to us much less severe than a beating with cane or whip, we must be very chary of using it even in adult dogs if we do not wish to intimidate them altogether.

In every kind of training which demands active co-operation on the part of the dog, as in jumping, retrieving, and other feats, we must not forget that even the best dog possesses no human sense of duty and, in sharp contrast to quite small children, will only collaborate as long as he is enjoying the work.

Correspondingly, punishment is here not only in-congruous but even harmful, since it is calculated to disgust the dog with this special activity, and to make him useless for it. It is only habit which causes a well-trained dog to retrieve a hare, follow a given trail or jump an obstacle if he is not 'in the mood'; there-fore, particularly at the beginning of such a training when the dog is not yet in the habit of obeying certain orders, his lesson should be limited to a few minutes and immediately stopped if his enthusiasm shows signs of waning. At all costs we must make the animal feel that he is not obliged but permitted to carry out the exercise in question.

After this short discourse on the general rules of training, let us return to the three special accomplish-ments which I strongly advise every owner to teach his dog. The salient one is, in my opinion, implicit obedience to the words 'Lie down', since it con-verts every dog into a much more desirable and useful companion. The animal must learn to lie down on command and not to move until recalled, and his ability to do this brings with it many advantages: the owner can leave the dog in any given place, such as outside a shop or house, so that the animal can nearly always accompany him and need rarely be left behind at home, a thing that implies the height of unhappiness to a really faithful dog. However the chief value of 'lying down' is an educational one, since it involves essential progress in obedience. It is asking much of a dog to expect him to conquer his urge to follow his master and to remain alone in some uncongenial place; and the exercise is equivalent to an unpleasant duty. Therefore the command to get up and follow comes as a happy release and he obeys joyfully, whereby 'coming when he is called' suddenly assumes the form of pleasure rather than of

work. Very often, the only way of making an intractable dog come when he is called is through the inter-
mediary stage of learning to 'lie down'. Egon von
Boyneburg, one of the best dog trainers I know, concentrated much more on 'Down' than on 'Come
here', in his training of gun dogs. He discovered
a method of stopping, in mid-chase, dogs which,
though normally obedient were such passionate
hunters that their lust made them deaf to their
master's whistle. He achieved this through an ex-
tension of the usual 'Down' training: the dogs were
taught to interrupt on command any activity whatever, even that of full chase, and to "lie down" and
'stay' until recalled. When a dog dashed off in
pursuit of game, Baron Boyneburg made no attempt
to recall him for the moment but simply cried with
appropriate loudness, 'Down'. Then one would see
a cloud of dust thrown up by sudden braking, and
after the cloud had dispersed, the figure of an
obediently recumbent dog.

The 'lying down' training is so easy that even
people with no special aptitude for such things
should be able to accomplish it. It should be started
between the seventh and eleventh month of a dog's
life, according to whether it belongs to a breed which
matures earlier or later. A too early start is bad, since
it is too much to ask of a quicksilvery, playful pup
that it should lie absolutely quiet to order; whereas
in an older, more staid dog much less resistance has
to be overcome in order to do so. The lessons should
be started on soft dry ground, a field for instance,
where the dog will not object to lying down, and here
he should be held firmly by neck and rump and
pressed gently to the ground to the accompanying
order of, 'Lie down' or other appropriate words
which the trainer has decided to use; a certain

amount of force may be necessary the first time the order is given. Some dogs understand the command earlier, others later, and still others stand stiff as a wooden horse and only begin to grasp the situation when first their hind-legs and then their fore-legs are bent under them by force.

These preliminary stages may appear somewhat comical to an outside observer but it is astonishing how few repetitions of them are required to make the dog understand the situation and lie down spontaneously when the order is given. From the very start the dog should be prevented from getting up before he is told. It is wrong to teach him to 'lie down' and to 'stay' in two separate lessons. First of all, one should stay very close to the dog, moving one's finger slightly just in front of his nose so that he gets no opportunity of getting up. Then one suddenly calls 'Come on', runs a few paces ahead and caresses or plays with him as requital for his recent ordeal. Should the dog show signs of tiring and of avoiding his master in order to prevent a repetition of the exercise, the lesson should be interrupted and postponed till the day following. The duration of time for 'staying' should only be very gradually increased, and the trainer must exercise no little tact in finding the happy medium between severity and friendliness.

The lesson must never decline into play—this must here be reserved as reward for an achievement —and a young dog must never be allowed to respond to the command by playfully throwing himself upon his back. On the other hand, one must take great pains to avoid disgusting the dog with the whole affair. When one has reached the stage where the dog will remain lying still for several minutes, one begins gradually to retreat from him, being careful at first not to move out of his sight, and when he is sufficiently familiar with this manoeuvre as to remain where he is for some minutes after his owner's departure from his side, one can then move out of sight. One can facilitate this trial for him by leaving by his side one or two of one's personal possessions, and the more articles one leaves and the bigger their size, the easier it will be for him to remain with them. If one takes one's dog camping and leaves him by the tent and blankets, he will, even if he has but a rudimentary idea of the foregoing lessons, remain by them for an indefinite period of time, waiting patiently for his master. Should a stranger attempt to purloin something, the dog will become half frenzied with anger, not because he has a real sense of his duty to protect his master's belongings, but because these objects infused with his master's smell symbolize for him the home which in some way they represent, and give him the guarantee that his master will sooner or later return to the place. Thus he is furious if anybody tries to remove them. And when one sees a well-trained dog apparently guarding his master's brief case, the psychological explanation is quite other than it appears to be. The article is in the dog's mind a somewhat reduced symbol of home; and the master has not left the dog there to guard the case, but the case to prevent the dog from departing.

An important point in this form of instruction, particularly when it is carried out in a neighbourhood strange to the dog, is the choice of a suitable place for him to 'lie down'. Before giving the command, one should always consider which place the dog himself would prefer if he were about to lie down to rest. It is cruel to make a dog lie down in the middle of a crowded footpath where there is no cover, for in such a place which, in his eyes, is entirely unsuitable for a rest, he will undergo mental

suffering, whereas he will feel quite content if ordered
to lie down in some quiet corner, preferably under
cover such as a seat. This rule should be the more
strictly observed because 'lying down' is a strenuous
task, which involves a considerable mental effort on
the part of the dog. Of course, a good and appro-
priately strict training of this sort is no cruelty to the
animal but, on the contrary implies an enrichment
of his life, since a well-trained dog can accompany
his master almost anywhere. In the case of very
intelligent dogs, the necessarily stringent laws of
training may be somewhat relaxed in the course
of time. Stasi, who was a past master in the art of
'lying down', knew quite well that I did not really
expect her to retain her sphinx-like pose indefinitely,
as the letter of the law demanded, when she was
guarding my bicycle. She lay down to order and
stayed in this posture to begin with, but if I watched
her secretly through a window I saw that she later
moved about within a radius of a few yards. But if
we were out visiting and I made her lie down in the
corner of the room, she would never attempt to get
up and move about in the same manner. In other
words she fully realized the reason for these actions.
In the end, and without any particular intention, we
arrived at the following compromise: when she was
made to lie down, in the absence of my bicycle or
brief-case, she waited for about ten minutes and, if I
did not reappear, she went home without me, but in
the presence of my belongings she would have waited
till the day of judgment.

Stasi attained such perfection in the art of lying
down on guard that, incredible though it may seem,
she would put herself on duty! While we were in
Posen, she had a litter of puppies, sired by the Dingo
at the Königsberg Zoo. (She was mated to this dog

after her union with the Siberian wolf had proved fruitless). A doctor friend lent me, or rather her, the kennel of his Alsatian which, unfortunately had just been stolen. Stasi remained three days by her puppies. On the fourth day, as I was about to leave the hospital where I was working, I found her there, lying beside my bicycle. Every attempt to return her to her children failed; she simply insisted on 'going on duty' again. Twice a day she ran to her children several streets away in order to feed them, but in half an hour she was back again lying beside my bicycle.

The second form of training, 'Basket', is the same thing in the house as 'lying down' outside. One may easily find the dog in the way and want to get rid of him for a time. The command 'Go away' is one that even the cleverest dog cannot understand, since 'away' is an abstract which he is quite unable to apprehend; one must tell him in a more concrete way whither one wishes him to go. The basket need not be a real one, but only means a fixed place to which the dog is made to retire on order, and which he must not leave without being told. It is best to choose some corner for which the dog has already shown a preference and to which he will always go willingly. Children and dogs can make themselves very unpopular by disturbing the conversation of adult people and a dog that has learned to leave people alone will certainly earn general approval. The same thing applies to children.

The third drill, which, likewise makes the dog a much pleasanter and less troublesome companion, is walking to 'heel'. Unfortunately, this extremely practical accomplishment, which makes a lead superfluous for a well trained dog, is harder to achieve than the two I have just described, and it

entails more frequent repetition if it is not to be forgotten. Teaching a dog to walk to heel consists simply of making him walk, on the lead, close by the left or right side of his master (the side must always be the same), keeping his head level with his master's legs, and accommodating his step to his master's pace. Few dogs will try to hold back when practising this exercise, but most of them tend to run too far forwards, a mistake which must be rectified each time by a jerk on the lead or a tap on the nose. Every time his master turns the dog must turn too, and this result is best attained by stooping somewhat and pressing the dog to one's side with the hand which is not holding the lead.

> *Nicht Kunst und Wissenchaft allein,*
> *Geduld muss bei dem Werke sein.*

The training involves many hours on the lead before the dog has learnt to walk satisfactorily to heel. Here, two orders must be complied with, calling the dog to heel and releasing him from it; in my experience the second is the hardest. In the case of 'Lie down', the releasing order, 'Come here' is easily intelligible to the dog and he soon learns not to move until it is given, but the command 'Go on' which releases the dog from heel is obviously not so easily understood. It is best, to begin with, to stand still, say 'Go on' and wait until he has done so. The dog must never be allowed to stray from heel on his own, otherwise he will imagine that this is permitted and will thus impair the training which has already been achieved. A further difficulty is that a clever dog soon notices whether it is on the lead or not and often ignores the command when the lead is first removed. It is therefore a good thing to accustom the animal from the start to a thin, light lead which he scarcely feels unless he is forcibly jerked back on it. The dog

apparently lacks an understanding of cause and effect in this connection, since in the early stages of her training Stasi responded to the command, 'Heel', when she had a lead on, whether I was holding it or not and no matter how far away she was from me. Without the lead she felt 'free' and did not respond to the command. Even well-trained dogs should be given an occasional 'refresher' on the lead. On the whole, however, just as in the case of 'lying down', the letter of the law may be somewhat relaxed when a dog has fully grasped the situation and has learned to carry out its orders with proficiency. Stasi, even as a young dog, soon forgot the meaning of the command, but this was of no consequence since it became quite unnecessary to give it: in any emergency she kept as perfectly to heel as any prize-winner at an obedience test. When traffic became dense she immediately came to heel of her own accord and there was never the least fear of losing her even in the enormous crowds that thronged the stations during the war; with the greatest exactitude, she followed my every footstep, the right side of her neck held close to my left knee.

She made touching use of this voluntary keeping to heel when she was in any particular temptation, as, for example, when we were walking through a crowded farm-yard and the clacking, fluttering hens and bleating lambs which thus expressed their consternation at the appearance of the red wolf, put her powers of self-control to sore trial. Then she pressed herself hard against my left knee to prevent her own fall; quivering with excitement, her nostrils extended and her ears cocked, she walked close beside me and I could see how strained was the invisible lead on which she had put herself. Of course, the dog could never have discovered this ingenious use for walking to heel had she not in her youth already mastered all the essential rules of the practice, but it pleases me to think that such a lesson, once learned, can be carried out by a dog not only with slavish exactitude but also in the form of a most sensible, one is almost tempted to say creative, variation.

5. CANINE CUSTOMS

Wi' social nose whyles snuff'd and snowkit.
BURNS: *The Twa Dogs*

THE ways in which social animals communicate
with each other, and the mechanisms which
guarantee the smooth co-operation of individuals
within the flock or pack, are completely different
from the word language which accomplishes these
vital functions in man. In *King Solomon's Ring*, I have
treated this subject comprehensively in the chapter
on the 'Language of animals'. The meaning of particular signals and of various expressive movements
and sounds is not determined by an individually
acquired convention, as is the case with human
words, but by innate instinctive norms of action and
reaction. The entire 'language' of an animal species
is therefore much more conservative and its customs
and usages incomparably more fixed and binding
than are those of man. One could write a whole book
on the inviolable laws governing canine ceremonial,
which determine the behaviour of stronger and
weaker, of dogs and bitches. Seen from without,
the effects of these laws, which are firmly anchored
to the hereditary behaviour pattern of the dog, closely

resemble the regulations of our own transmitted human customs. This also applies to the effects of these laws on social life, and it is in the sense of this analogy that the chapter heading is to be understood.

Nothing is more tedious than an abstract enunciation of laws, however interesting they may be in themselves; I shall therefore avoid abstractions and try, in a series of everyday examples, so to depict the living effects of the social regulations of canine life that the reader will automatically arrive at the theory of these laws. I will turn first to the behaviour associated with ranking order, whose age-old customs and usages not only express but also very largely determine social superiority and inferiority. Let us consider a series of canine encounters such as my readers will often have seen for themselves.

*   *   *   *

Wolf and I are walking down the lane. As we pass the village pump and turn into the main road, we suddenly see Wolf's traditional enemy and rival, Rolf, standing in the middle of the road about two hundred yards away from us. We have to pass him, so a meeting is unavoidable. These two dogs which are the strongest and most feared, in other words the highest in rank in the village, cordially detest one another but at the same time are imbued with so much mutual respect that, so far as I know, they have never come to blows. Both of them seem to view this particular encounter with equal antipathy. From within their respective gardens they would bark and threaten furiously, each convinced that only the fence prevented him from flying at the other's throat. But now their emotions are different and, anthropomorphizing somewhat, I interpret

them thus: each dog feels that he must keep up his prestige by putting his former threats into action and fears that it would be 'losing face' not to do so. They have, of course, seen each other from afar and immediately assume an attitude of self-display, that is, they stiffen up and raise their tails vertically on high, walking more and more slowly as they approach each other. When they are separated by a mere fifteen yards or so, Rolf suddenly lies down like a crouching tiger. Neither face shows a sign of hesitation or of threatening. Foreheads and noses show no wrinkles, ears are erect and pointing forwards, eyes are wide open. Wolf reacts in no way to the crouching attitude of Rolf, no matter how threatening the latter appears to a human eye, but, walking inflexibly up to his rival, stands still by his side. Thereupon Rolf shoots up to his full height and now the two stand flank to flank, head to tail sniffing each other's freely proffered hindquarters. This voluntary rendering of the anal regions is the expression of self-assurance and if this is at all reduced the tail sinks immediately; one can read by its angle, as by an indicator, the level of courage in the dog.

The two animals hold this tense position for some time, then, gradually, the smooth faces begin to pucker: the foreheads are furrowed by horizontal and vertical lines directed towards a point above the eyes; the noses are wrinkled, the fangs bared. These facial expressions are obviously threatening, and are displayed also by dogs which are frightened and threaten in self-defence when cornered. The extent of the dog's own morale and control of the situation is indicated by two parts of the head only: the ears and the corners of the mouth. If the former are directed upwards and forwards and the latter are drawn well forward, the dog is unafraid and may

attack at any moment. Every vestige of fear expresses itself in a corresponding movement of the ears and the corners of the mouth, as though the unseen powers which aid flight were pulling the animal backwards. The threatening attitude is accompanied by growling; the deeper the growls the more sure of itself the animal feels—allowing, of course, for the individual tone of voice: a cheeky fox-terrier will obviously growl on a higher note than a timorous St Bernard.

Still flank to flank, Rolf and Wolf now begin to circle round each other. Every moment I expect the start of hostilities, but the absolute balance of power prevents the declaration of war. The growls become more ominous but still nothing happens. I have a vague suspicion, enhanced by the sidelong glances which first Wolf and then Rolf throw at me that they are not only expecting but indeed hoping that I will separate them and so absolve them from the moral duty of a fight. The urge to preserve prestige and dignity is not specifically human, but lies deep into the instinctive layers of the mind which, in the higher animals, are closely related to our own.

I do not interfere but leave it to the dogs to find a dignified way out. Very slowly they separate and walk, step by step to opposite corners of the road. Finally, still watching each other out of the corner of one eye, they lift a hind leg, simultaneously, as though at an order, Wolf against a telegraph post, Rolf against the fence. Then, in an attitude of self-display, they proceed on their own ways, each priding himself on having gained a moral victory and intimidated the other.

Bitches behave in a peculiar way when they are present at a meeting of two dogs equal in strength and rank. On such occasions, Wolf's wife, Susi,

certainly hopes for a fight; not that she helps her husband actively but she likes to see him thrash an opponent. I have twice watched her adopt a most deceitful ruse in order to achieve this end: Wolf was standing head to tail with another dog—each time it was an outsider, a 'summer visitor'—and Susi prowled round them carefully and interestedly, the dogs in the meantime taking no notice of her as a bitch. Then, silently but vigorously, she nipped her husband in his hindquarters, which were presented to the foe. Wolf assumed that the latter, by an intolerable breach of all the age-old laws of canine custom, had bitten his posterior whilst sniffing it, and fell on him immediately. Since the attack appeared to the other dog an equally unforgivable contravention, the ensuing battle was unusually grim.

*   *   *   *

Wolf meets an aged mongrel which lives at one of the houses at the very top of our village. Before he was grown up he used to be very much afraid of the old fellow; now he is so no longer but he hates him more than any other dog and never misses an opportunity of letting him know it. As the dogs see each other, the older one stiffens up immediately but Wolf rushes at him, bumping him hard with his shoulder and with a slinging movement of his hindquarters; then he stops still beside him. The old dog has snapped viciously at his foe, but his teeth close in mid-air, his intentions being thwarted by the impact of Wolf's body. He is now standing quite still stiffly drawn up to his full height, but his tail is low for he cannot bring himself to offer his hind parts confidently. His nose and forehead are wrinkled threateningly, his head, held low, is stretched forward. This attitude, which is accompanied by angry

growling, appears most ominous and, as Wolf again tries to approach, the old dog makes a desperate snapping movement in his direction, whereupon Wolf recoils somewhat. Stiff-legged, with an exaggerated pompous gait, Wolf circles round his enemy, then he lifts his leg against the nearest appropriate object and retires. The feelings of the old dog, if put into words, might be expressed as follows: 'I am no rival for you; I have no wish to be your social equal or superior; I will not encroach on your territory. All I ask is that you should leave me alone. But if you will not do so then I will fight with all available means, whether fair or unfair.' But what are Wolf's feelings?

*   *   *   *

By the village pump Wolf meets a little yellow mongrel which, in mortal terror, seeks to escape through the open door of the local stores. Wolf pursues him hotly, impinging broadsides on him and bumping him with the slinging movement I have just described, thereby catapulting the little dog from the shop on to the street. Wolf is upon him like a thunderbolt, bumping him again and again. The little dog yells each time as if in great pain and finally he snaps and bites desperately at his assailant. Wolf produces neither a growl nor a threatening grimace but, ignoring the bites, calmly goes on with his bumping. So thoroughly does he despise the other as an opponent that he does not even find it worth while opening his mouth. But he hates the yellow dog, which has repeatedly appeared in our garden when Susi has been in season and he now vents his indignation on it in this vulgar manner. The kind of fear which expresses itself in cries of pain before the actual pain is felt is characterized in dogs by a definite position of the corners of the mouth:

these are pulled so far back that the mucous membrane of the buccal cavity is rolled outwards and becomes visible as a dark frame to the lips. Even by human standards, the canine face is thus invested with a peculiar whining expression much in keeping with the accompanying sounds.

Wolf I visits his wife Senta and their grown-up children on the terrace in front of our house. He greets Senta, both wag their tails and she licks him affectionately on the corners of his mouth, pushing him fondly with her nose. Then Wolf turns to one of his sons, who approaches his father gladly, shoves him with his nose but frustrates his attempts to sniff his hind quarters by drawing his persistently wagging tail between his legs. The young dog's back is arched, his bearing servile, nevertheless he exhibits no fear of his father, indeed he importunes him with constant nuzzling and attempts to lick the corners of his mouth. The old dog does not take on a self-assertive attitude but holds himself in such a stiff and dignified posture as to appear almost embarrassed: he turns his head to one side away from the muzzle of the licking pup and raises his nose high out of range. As the young dog, encouraged by this withdrawal, becomes more assiduous, a slight crease of disapproval crosses the father's face. The forehead of the young dog, on the other hand, is not only smooth but so widely stretched that the retracted angles of the eyes appear slit-like and depressed. As was also the case with Senta's manner of greeting Wolf I, the expressional movements of the pup are exactly similar to those with which a very obedient dog greets its master. Anthropomorphically speaking, the young dog has found a compromise between a certain degree of fear and the love which urges him to approach his superior.

*   *   *   *

In the village Susi meets a big, cross-bred Collie-Alsatian about one year old and a son of the above mentioned Rolf. For a moment, mistaking her for Wolf, of whom he is terrified, he takes fright.

Owing to their poor eyesight, dogs can only distinguish rough outlines of objects at a distance, and since Wolf is the only Chow local dogs are used to seeing about the district, Susi is occasionally mistaken for her formidable relative. The impertinence which this young female early developed is certainly attributable to the general deference which she inspires as a result of this error and which she evidently ascribes to her own ferocity. It is interesting to see how little colour sense the domestic dog has, for Wolf and Susi are often mistaken for each other although Wolf is red and Susi blue-grey in colour.

To return to our anecdote, the young dog flees but is quickly overtaken and held up by Susi. As he stands humbly before her with lowered ears and widely distended forehead, the scarcely eight months old bitch begins to wag her tail superciliously. She tries to sniff his hind parts but he shyly draws his tail between his legs and whips round, presenting to her not his hind quarters, but only his breast and head. And now he seems to notice for the first time that he is not dealing with the dreaded male but with a pleasant young female. He stretches up his neck, raises his tail and advances with a dancing action of his fore-paws. In spite of these signs of assertiveness, his face and ears still express social deference, but this gradually subsides giving place to an expression which I shall term the 'politeness look', and which only differs from the 'deference look' in the position of the ears and the corners of the mouth: the former are still laid back and flattened but they are now sometimes pressed so tightly together that the points

are in contact; the latter are drawn back as in the deference look but instead of being dragged complainingly downwards they have a definite upward tilt, producing, for the human observer, an expression akin to laughing. When this expressive movement is clearly marked, an invitation to play always follows; here the slightly opened jaws which reveal the tongue, and the tilted angles of the mouth which stretches almost from ear to ear give a still stronger impression of laughing. This 'laughing' is most often seen in dogs playing with an adored master and which become so excited that they soon start panting. Perhaps these facial movements are preliminary signs of the panting which sets in as the playing mood gains ascendancy. The inference is supported by the fact that in erotically tinged play dogs frequently 'laugh' and become so heated after even moderate exertion that they start panting heavily. The dog now confronting Susi laughs more and more and dances harder with his fore-paws. Suddenly he springs against the little bitch, pushing her in the breast with his fore-paws then he twists round and dashes off, holding himself in a special and peculiar way: his back is still arched deferentially, his hindquarters drawn in under his body, and his tail is pressed between his legs. Yet in this timid attitude, he executes leaps of friendly playfulness and his tail wags as far as his hind legs will allow. He stops his flight after a few yards, when he hurls himself round again and stands before the bitch with a broad grin on his face. He has now raised his tail high enough to prevent his hocks from hindering its joyful wagging which is no longer limited to the tail itself but includes the back half of the body as well. Again he springs against Susi and this time his overtures have undoubtedly a slightly erotic character,

which however remain symbolic since the bitch is not on heat.

*   *   *   *

At Schloss Altenberg, the home of a huge, coal-black Newfoundland called Lord, the small daughter of the house received on her birthday a charming little dwarf Pinscher barely two months old. I witnessed the first meeting of these animals. Although Quick, the Pinscher, was an uppish little fellow, he got the fright of his life when he saw the mountain of black fur advancing towards him and, like all puppies in such a predicament, he rolled over on his back ejecting a minute yellow fountain as the big dog nosed at his belly. After sniffing at this emotional outflow, Lord turned slowly and ponderously away from the aghast puppy. Next moment, however, Quick was on his feet again, and now he rushed, like a non-stop automaton, in small figures of eight in and out of the Newfoundland's feet. At the same time he jumped playfully up at him, inviting him to follow. The tearful little owner who, in the meantime had only been held back from intervening by her hard-hearted brothers, breathed a sigh of relief as the encounter developed into the truly moving spectacle of a very big dog playing with a very little one.

*   *   *   *

I have chosen these six canine encounters as examples because of their distinctive character. In actual fact, there are of course innumerable transitions and combinations between the emotions and corresponding expressive movements of self-assurance and fear, of self-display and deference, of attack and defence. This makes the analysis of behaviour reactions very difficult, and one must be very familiar with the types of expression I have described

—and many others too—to identify them in the dog's face, where at times they are only partially discernible and at other times only to be seen mingled with others.

*   *   *   *

There is one particularly endearing canine habit, which has been fixed since early times in the hereditary characters of the central nervous system of the dog. This is the chivalrous treatment of females and puppies. No normal male will bite a female of its species; the bitch is absolutely taboo and can treat a dog as she likes, nipping or even seriously biting him. The dog has at his disposal no means of retaliation other than deferential gestures and the 'politeness look', with which he may attempt to divert the attacks of the bitch into play. Masculine dignity forbids the only other outlet—flight—for dogs are always at great pains to 'keep face' in front of bitches. In the wolf, as also in all predominantly wolf-blooded Greenland dogs, this chivalrous self-control is extended only to females of his own pack; in all preponderantly Jackal dogs, it applies to every bitch, even if she is a complete stranger. The Chow holds an intermediate position: if he always lives with his own kind, he may behave loutishly towards strange jackal bitches though I have never known one that actually bit them.

If I required another proof of the basic zoological difference between dogs with a strong wolf strain and our ordinary European breeds, I should point to the enmity which can regularly be observed to exist between these two types, which originate from two different wild forms. The spontaneous hate which a Chow evokes amongst village dogs which have never seen one before, and conversely, the readiness with which any mongrel will accept a jackal or a dingo as one of his own kind, are to me far more convincing arguments for the distinction than all the measurements and calculations of cranial and skeletal proportions on whose statistical results the contrary opinion has been based. My own opinion is strengthened by certain anomalies of social behaviour: members of opposite types often do not recognize each other so that males fail to respect the most commonplace 'canine rights' of bitches and puppies. The research worker in behaviour, the zoologist, who has any fine feeling for systematic and genealogical coherence, can see that the Lupus dog is of a different species from the Jackal one. And since dogs themselves, which are certainly not influenced by scientific controversy, undoubtedly see the same thing, I believe them more implicitly than any statistics.

Amongst canines belonging to the same species and the same social union, a young one of less than about six months old is absolutely inviolable. The gesture of humiliation—rolling over and urinating—is only necessary in the first instant of meeting when it apparently serves the purpose of informing the older dog that he is dealing with a pup. Owing to lack of observations and experiments, I am unable to say for certain whether the adult dog recognizes the helplessness of infancy by this mechanism only or whether the smell of the pup also helps him to diagnose its tender age. Certainly the relation in size between old and young plays no part in this recognition. A bad-tempered fox-terrier treats a young St Bernard as a helpless baby even if it is twice his size; and, conversely, male dogs of large breeds have no inhibitions about fighting adult dogs of small breeds even though this seems most unchivalrous from a human point of view. I will not entirely impugn the chivalry towards little dogs so often attributed to St Bernards, Newfoundlands and Great Danes but I myself have never met with such a noble animal in all my large circle of canine acquaintances.

An uncommonly entertaining and even moving scene can be produced if one unkindly gives a dignified male dog, addicted to self-display, to a litter of young pups 'to play with'. Our old Wolf I was specially fitted for this experiment; he was very serious and not at all playful; thus it caused him much embarrassment when he was forced to pay visits to his two month old children and their dingo foster-brother on the terrace. Young dogs of five months and over have a certain respect for the professorial dignity of an old canine male but in still younger puppies this sentiment is entirely lacking. They fall upon their father, nipping his legs with their needle-sharp, remorseless little teeth, whereupon he gingerly lifts one foot after the other as though he had trodden on something hot. The poor martyr may not even growl, far less punish one of his troublesome offspring. After a while our querulous Wolf let himself be cajoled into playing with his children, but he never voluntarily went on to the terrace while they were small.

A dog finds himself in a rather similar situation when confronted with an attacking bitch. The inhibition against biting or even growling is the same, but the motive which bids him approach the aggressive female is incomparably stronger and the conflict between male dignity, fear of his assailant's sharp teeth and the power of his erotic drives, lead to a type of behaviour which sometimes appears like a satire on the human being. It is chiefly the playful part, the 'politeness behaviour' I have just described, which makes an old dog appear so awkward. When

such a rough customer who has long outgrown his playfulness, makes declarations of love by marking time with his fore-feet and bounding backwards and forwards, even the non-anthropomorphizing observer cannot help drawing certain comparisons; these are enhanced by the behaviour of the bitch, which treats the dog with much arrogance, knowing that he has got to put up with anything.

I once saw a good example of this behaviour when, together with Stasi, I visited the grey wolf in his cage. I shall describe the encounter more fully later on. After a short while, the wolf invited me to play and I, feeling flattered, accepted. But Stasi felt slighted because I took more notice of the wolf than of her and she suddenly attacked my partner in the game. Now Chow bitches have a particularly nasty, nagging bark and a special way of nipping when they wish to punish a male dog: they do not bite hard and deep like fighting males; they apparently only seize the skin, but vigorously enough to make the male howl with pain. The wolf, too, howled, attempting at the same time to placate Stasi by attitudes of deference and gestures of politeness. Naturally I did not wish to put his chivalry to the test for fear that I myself should have to suffer the consequences, so I sternly adjured the angry female to silence. And so paradoxically I had to rebuke Stasi to prevent her from injuring the good-natured wolf. Only ten minutes earlier, I had set in readiness outside the cage an iron bar and two buckets of water to save my precious Stasi in case the great beast of prey attacked her. 'Sic transit gloria—lupi!'

6. MASTER AND DOG

PEOPLE are prompted to keep animals by many different motives and not all of them are good ones. Amongst passionate lovers of animals, particularly dog-lovers, there is a special category of unhappy people who, through bitter experience, have lost faith in mankind and seek refuge with animals. It makes me sad and pensive to hear the fallacy, 'Animals are so much better than people'. This is not really the case. Admittedly, the fidelity of a dog is a thing whose counterpart is not so easily found amongst the social loyalties of man, but then the dog has no knowledge of the labyrinths of often opposing moral obligations, he only knows in minute measure the conflict between inclination and obligation, in other words, he is ignorant of all that leads us poor human beings into sin. Seen from the viewpoint of human responsibilities, even the most faithful dog is to a large extent amoral. Extensive knowledge of the social behaviour of the higher animals does not, as so many think, make one under-estimate the differences between man and animal. I maintain, on the contrary, that only somebody who is really familiar with animal behaviour is able to appreciate the unique and exalted position held by man in the world of living creatures. For he is

> *the master work, the end*
> *Of all yet done; a creature who not prone*
> *And brute as other creatures, but imbued*
> *With sanctity of reason.*

The scientific comparison of man and animals which forms such a large part of our research methods no more implies a lowering of human dignity than does the recognition of the origin of species. The essence of creative organic evolution is that it produces completely new and higher characters which were in no way indicated or even implicit in the preceding stage from which they took their origin. Of course, even to-day, the animal is still present in man, but never man in the animal. Our genealogical examination methods which necessarily proceed from the lowest step, from the animal, enable us to see in clear relief the essentially human, the high achievements of human reason and ethics which have never existed in the animal world. They stand out clearly against the background of older historical properties and capacities which man has in common with the higher animals even to-day. The assertion that animals are better than man is sheer blasphemy; for the critical research biologist, who does not lightly take the name of God in vain, such a statement means the satanic denial of creative development in the world of living organisms.

Unfortunately, a deplorably large number of animal lovers, particularly those concerned with animal protection, harbour this ethically dangerous point of view. Only that kind of love for animals is beautiful and edifying which arises from the broader and more general love of the whole world of living creatures, a love whose most important and central feature must always be the love of mankind. Only people who feel this may give their affection to animals without moral danger. The human being who, disappointed and embittered by human weakness, removes his love from mankind and bestows it on dogs and cats is committing a grave sin, a repulsive social

perversion. Hatred of humanity and love of animals
make a very bad combination. Of course it is
harmless and legitimate for a lonely person, who,
for some reason or other is deprived of social intercourse to procure a dog to assuage an inward
longing to love and be loved, for it is a fact that one
no longer feels alone in the world when there is
at least one being who is pleased at one's return
home.

The study of the harmonious concord between
master and dog is extraordinarily instructive from
the point of view of both animal and human psycho-
logy and it is sometimes quite entertaining as well.
Much is often revealed by the sort of dog chosen, and
still more by the relationship which later develops
between master and charge. Just as in human relations, here too complete disparity as well as strong
resemblance often lead to mutual happiness. In older
married couples, one often discovers features which
give man and wife the semblance of brother and
sister; in the same way, one may notice in a master
and a dog who have spent some time together likenesses in manner which are touching and comical at
the same time. In the case of experienced dog
owners, these likenesses are accentuated by the choice
of a particular breed or individual dog, since this is
usually determined by personal sympathy for related
characteristics. The Chow bitches, which have been
the successive companions of my wife, are typical
examples of such 'sympathy' or 'resonance' dogs.
The same applies in principle to myself, and friends
who know both ourselves and our dogs really well
often amuse themselves by finding in our dogs the
reflection of our own personalities. My wife's dogs
are always particularly cleanly and have a certain
sense of order. Apparently without any prompting

they never walk through puddles and they move along the narrowest paths between flower and vegetable beds without setting foot on either. But my dogs, alas, roll in any filth and bring enormous quantities of dirt into the house; in short the difference between our dogs is analogous with the difference between my wife and myself. This can partly be explained by the fact that my wife always picks from our litters only those young dogs in which the inheritance of the 'nobler', more reticent, cleaner and almost feline Chow-Chow predominates while I have always preferred those with the livelier, more vital, but certainly more vulgar nature of my old Alsatian, Tito. A further parallel lies in the fact that, despite the closest blood-relationship, my wife's dogs eat moderately and delicately, while mine are disgustingly greedy. But how that comes about I am at a loss to explain.

In my opinion, owning a parallel or resonance dog gives one a feeling of balance or even of self-satisfaction. Such a relationship between man and dog is supported by the sense that both are 'at peace with themselves'. The situation is different in the case of the typological opposite of the resonance dog, an example of which I saw in the street the other day. A pale, narrow-chested man with a worried and irritable expression, his apparel of a shabby respectability, complete with pince-nez, in fact, every inch a clerk, was walking along with a large, rather under-fed-looking Alsatian which slunk in a subdued way at his heels. The man carried a heavy whip and, as he suddenly stopped and the dog advanced a few inches beyond the permitted line, he aimed a blow at its nose with the handle of the whip. As he did so, his face registered such abysmal hate and nervous irritability that I could hardly restrain myself from interfering and starting a public quarrel. I bet a thousand to one that the luckless dog played the same role in the life of his still more luckless master as the latter in the life of his perhaps equally pitiable superior at the office.

7. DOGS AND CHILDREN

None other cared to try thy strength,
And hurl thee sidelong at full length.
But we well knew each other's mind
And paid our little debts in kind.

W. S. LANDOR

I WAS unlucky in having a dogless childhood. My mother belonged to the generation which had just discovered bacteria, when most children of well-to-do-families contracted rickets because people were so afraid of bacteria that they sterilized all the milk vitamins to death. It was only when I reached years of discretion and enough reliance could be placed on my manly word of honour not to let myself be licked by the animal, that I was finally allowed to have my first dog; and this unfortunately was a complete idiot of a dog which, for a long time, deprived me of any further wish to possess another. In another chapter I have told you in more detail about this characterless creature, the dachshund Kroki.

My own children have grown up in the closest companionship with dogs: we had five of them when they were small. I can still see the little mites crawling on all fours beneath the belly of the big Alsatian, to the indescribable horror of my poor mother. When my son was learning to walk he used to hang on to

Tito's long tail to pull himself up and change over from the four-legged to the two-legged method of locomotion. Tito kept still with the patience of a saint but as soon as the child was standing upright and had let go of her sorely-tried tail, she would wag it with relief so hard that it generally banged into some part of his anatomy and knocked him off his feet all over again.

Sensitive dogs are particularly gentle with the children of a beloved master; it is as though they understand how much they mean to him. And fear that the dog might harm the children is quite absurd, on the contrary, there is a danger that the dog, by being too tolerant of the children, may educate them to roughness and inconsideration. One must be on one's guard against this; particularly in the case of the large and very good-natured breeds, such as St Bernards, Newfoundlands. In general, however, dogs know very well how to escape the attentions of children when they become tiresome—a fact of great educational value: since normal children derive much pleasure from the company of dogs and are correspondingly disappointed when they run away from them, they soon realize how they must behave in order to make themselves desirable companions from the dog's point of view. Children with a certain amount of natural tact thus learn at a very tender age the value of consideration for others.

When I notice, in somebody else's house, that the dog does not recoil from the five or six year old child but instead approaches him without any shyness, my opinion of the child and of the whole family rises. Unfortunately, the farm children of my own immediate neighbourhood are far too rough for any dealings with dogs. In our neighbourhood, you never see a group of small boys, accompanied by one or more

dogs. I know, of course, individual farm children who are kind to their own dogs, but in a larger crowd of boys there always seems to be at least one bully amongst them who makes the rest follow his example. At any rate, the average Lower Austrian dog flees at the approach of the average Lower Austrian boy. This need not be the case and is not everywhere so. In White Russia, for example, one regularly sees mixed gangs of boys and dogs wandering through the villages, usually flaxenheaded boys of five to seven years old and innumerable dogs of uncertain breed. The dogs have no fear of the boys but the greatest confidence in them. And from this confidence, one can draw far-reaching conclusions about the propensities of those boys' characters. It is certainly a strong inherent affinity with nature that makes them so gentle with their animals.

The most amazing friendship between a dog and a child that I ever knew—I was, at the time, myself a child—concerned an enormous coal-black Newfoundland and my future brother-in-law, Peter Pflaum, respectively watch-dog and son of the neighbouring mansion, Schloss Altenberg. Lord, as the Newfoundland was called, was a dog of truly ideal temperament, brave to the point of rashness, faithful and intelligent and of amazing integrity of character. Peter was, as he will boast to this day, not without a certain amount of justifiable pride, a thoroughly naughty boy. And it was this eleven-year-old boy that the huge creature chose as master when he arrived in Altenberg as a full-grown dog one and a half years old. What made him do this is still not clear to me, for he belonged to that type of dog which commonly attaches itself to a grown-up man, usually to the head of the family. Perhaps chivalrous motives impelled him to it, for Peter was the smallest and

weakest not only of four brothers but of the whole
wild gang of many boys and a few girls who made
the Altenberg woods unsafe by their Red Indian
pranks whose cracks and explosions were not only
realistic but often real. In the course of our games
we each frequently got beaten up by the others, Peter
most frequently of all, and, as I contend, deservedly.
But let a boy try hitting another when a dog,
massive as a lion and black as the night, at once lays
two heavy paws on the shoulder of the offender,
bares huge, snow-white teeth under his very nose,
and growls threateningly in tones deep as organ
pipes. Peter rewarded this loyalty with heartfelt devotion, and the two were quite inseparable. This
impeded Peter's education somewhat, for even Herr
Niedermaier, the strict house tutor of the fatherless
boy dared not so much as raise his voice against
Peter, for, should he do so, an ominous rumbling,
deep as thunder, would reverberate from a corner
and the black lion would stroll up majestically;
whereupon Herr Niedermaier would shrug his
shoulders helplessly and turn away.

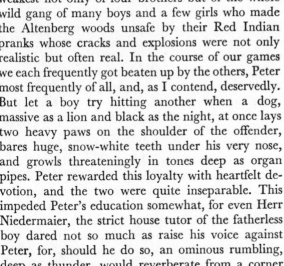

My mother told me of a similar case in her parents'
home where a great, strong Leonberger, likewise a
member of one of the largest breeds of dog, adopted
as mistress the youngest sister, who, like Peter, was a
child 'sat on' by many elder brothers and sisters.

I have a prejudice against people, even very small
children, who are afraid of dogs. This prejudice is
quite unjustified for it is a completely normal reaction for a small person, at the first sight of such a
large beast of prey, at first to be anxious and careful.
But the contrary standpoint, that I love children
that show no fear even of big, strange dogs and know
how to handle them properly, has its justification, for
this can only be done by someone who possesses a

certain understanding of nature and of our fellow beings. My own children were, long before the end of
their first year, such complete 'doggy people', that
it would never have entered their heads that a dog
could harm them. And for this very reason, my
daughter Agnes before she had quite reached the age
of six years, once gave me a terrible fright. It happened in this way: She and her brother once came
back from a walk accompanied by a large, very good-
looking Alsatian which had joined them. I guessed
it to be six or seven years old and was later proved
to be right. This dog followed the children home,
keeping very close to them and walking to heel. He
seemed rather subdued and only let me stroke him
under protest, that is by wrinkling his lips slightly,
but he clung with a strange persistence to the two
children. The whole thing was uncanny to me. The
dog seemed slightly unbalanced mentally, and why
on earth had he so suddenly attached himself to the
children? This found a very natural explanation later
on: the dog was a very nervous, gun-shy animal.
He lived in a village about eight miles upstream,
and, at the rather noisy celebrations of the local
church festival, he had taken fright at the shooting in
the side-shows, and run away so far that he had been
unable to find his way home. His owner had two
children whom he adored and who were not unlike
mine in age and appearance. This was obviously
why he had attached himself to my two when he met
them. At the time, however, I did not know all this
and it was with mixed feelings that I consented
when the children begged me to let them keep him
should the owner not turn up. They were, of course,
flattered by this big and beautiful dog that clung to
them so tenaciously.

The matter was further complicated by the fact

that our own dog, Wolf I, was also extremely attached to the children in the more independent and self-sufficient manner of a male Lupus dog. It was understandable that this obsequious slave, this confounded interloper, who usurped his place in the favours of the children, injured Wolf's pride horribly. My meaning threats, directed equally at both dogs, and the still subdued and timorous aspect of the newcomer were sufficient at first to prevent a battle, but on the whole I was not enthusiastic about this new acquisition.

The eruption was inevitable. I had retired to a small room beyond the bathroom at the top of the house. Presently my peaceful meditations were disturbed by the sounds of a terrible dog-fight and in the midst of it—oh, horror!—piercing cries for help from my little Agnes! I precipitated myself down the stairs, hanging on to my trousers with one hand, and saw in front of the house the hair-raising spectacle of the two dogs locked in bitter fight and protruding from beneath them—the legs of my little daughter. I rushed up like a madman, seized the neck of a dog in either hand and tore them apart with superhuman strength, thereby revealing the little girl. She was lying on her back and she too had one hand firmly fixed on each of the dogs' necks, in the attempt to wrest them apart. She now told me that, sitting on the ground between them, she had begun to stroke both dogs together with the object, as she thought, of reconciling them. Naturally, this had the opposite effect and the two animals flew at each other's throats. Agnes had tried to hold them apart and had not let go even when she was thrown on the ground and trampled underfoot. It had never for a second occurred to her that either of them could harm her!

8. CHOOSING A DOG

How shall I know if I do choose the right?
SHAKESPEARE: *Merchant of Venice*

MAKING up one's mind is always difficult, especially when getting a dog, for there are so many different breeds to choose from; and an adviser can only give counsel if he is acquainted with the prospective owner and knows what he expects of his dog. For example, a sentimental and lonely old spinster seeking an object on which to lavish all her affection and care would find little consolation in the aloof personality of a Chow, which disdains physical caresses and only greets its returning mistress with a supercilious wag of its tail instead of jumping up like other dogs. To anybody wanting a dog of affectionate nature, a creature which, with its head on its master's knee will lift up its amber eyes and gaze at him in blind devotion for hours on end, I should recommend a Red Setter or a dog of a similar long-haired, long-eared breed. Personally I find these dogs too sentimental. To-day, with our troubled minds and the awful threat of atom warfare hanging over us we have reason enough to be sad, and continual contact with a being which has the same sort of temperament and which from time to time makes its presence felt by a deep if gentle sigh, is probably not desirable for many of us. The sad or cheerful mood of one friend can greatly influence another, and a person of equable or vivacious temperament can be a real inspiration for his surroundings. The same applies to a cheerful dog and I think that the great popularity enjoyed by some comical breeds of dog is largely attributable to our longing for gaiety. A Sealyham's love of fun, and his fidelity to his master can prove a real moral support to a melancholy type of person. Who can help laughing when such an amusing little creature, bursting with the joys of life, comes bouncing along on his far too short legs (walking teats, as a Sealyham-owning friend of mine calls them), cocks his head and, with an expression half-knowing and half innocent, looks up at his master inviting him to play?

To the person seeking not only a personal friend but also a piece of unwarped nature, I recommend a fundamentally different type of dog. I myself prefer dogs not too far removed from the wild form. My Chow-Alsatian cross-breds are very close to their wild ancestors, both in their physical and mental properties. The less a dog has become altered in type by domestication, the more he has retained the properties of the wild predator, the more wonderful his friendship seems to me. For this reason, I dislike spoiling too much of a dog's true nature by training and I should not even wish my dogs to lose the savage hunting urge that has caused me so much trouble and expense. Were they gentle lambs incapable of hurting a fly it would seem to me less wonderful that I can trust my children to them without a care. An alarming event first made me realize this. One day, during a hard winter, a deer crossed our snowed-up garden fence and was torn to pieces by my three dogs. As I stood horror-stricken by the mutilated corpse I became conscious of the unconditional faith which I placed in the social inhibition of these blood-thirsty beasts, for my children were at that time smaller and more defenceless than the deer whose gory remains lay before me in the snow. I was myself astonished at the absolute fearlessness with which I daily entrusted the fragile limbs of my children to the wolf-like jaws.

It is very unusual indeed for a dog to attack his master's children and I do not think it ever happens in mentally healthy dogs. However, in nervous and high-bred dogs, but occasionally even in mongrels, jealousy, to which all dogs are very prone, can cause horrible effects. I have lately heard of the truly shocking case of a cross-bred terrier which, up to that time had been the pampered darling of the family, but had been chained up after the arrival of a baby. At the first opportunity he jumped into its pram and killed it. Happily it is rare that jealousy reaches such a dangerous pitch and it seems that it only does so in the more infantile type of dog. The wolf dogs that I fancy were never jealous of the babies, but, on the contrary, adopted a more or less parental attitude towards them. And perhaps this is one of the reasons why I am so fond of that type of dog.

But this is all a matter of taste and I quite realize that my wild, predatory dog is not every man's choice. Lupus-blooded dogs are not easy to train, owing to their sensibility, their exclusiveness and their independence of character, and only somebody who knows and understands these dogs can exploit the incredible resources of their minds, and derive real pleasure from them. Others will obtain more enjoyment from a good honest Boxer or from an Airedale Terrier, in the same way as a beginner in photography will achieve more success with a simple

box camera than with a highly complicated apparatus.

This does not mean that I deprecate the mentally uncomplicated dog; on the contrary, I am very fond of Boxers and the large terriers whose plucky and affectionate dispositions can hardly be spoiled even by clumsy trainers. I must also point out that my remarks on the general characteristics of individual dog breeds only apply generally, since every possible exception to the rule occurs; fundamentally such a generalization is just as fallible as would be an all-round description of the English, the French or the Germans. I know very sensitive Boxers, and Chows completely lacking in character; I have even known a most resolute and independent spaniel. My blue-coloured Susi, whose Alsatian lineage admittedly has much influence on her character, shows captivating friendliness to friends of my family and is certainly in no way so aloof as other Chows.

It is perhaps more necessary to advise the beginner which dogs not to keep, and which proclivities in a future pet he should steer clear of, than to give him any positive advice. But before I go further with these warnings it must be understood that their object is not to deter anybody from keeping a dog. Any dog is better than none and even if the beginner infringes all the rules here set down, he will still gain a lot of pleasure from his dog. But his pleasure will be greater if he complies with my precepts, the first one of which is: buy only a dog which is healthy in mind and body. In the absence of good reasons for other choice, take the strongest, fattest and liveliest pup of the litter, three properties which concur with remarkable regularity. Bitches are of course slighter than dogs, which fact must be considered at the time. Should parents or offspring show any signs of decadence, it is better to refuse a pup. Particular care must be exercised in the case of foreign breeds which, outside their country of origin, are often too highly inbred owing to paucity of good specimens. Better a dog of lesser pedigree (a certificate usually left lying about in some drawer at home) and a more vital, less highly strung animal. As I shall explain in the chapter, 'An Appeal to Dog Breeders', I have such a poor opinion of modern dog-breeding, with its over-estimation of 'beauty' and neglect of intelligence, that I am inclined to advise a beginner not to buy a dog with too 'good' a pedigree. One is probably less likely to obtain in a mongrel a nervous, mentally deficient animal than in a dog with eight champions in its pedigree. An Alsatian should always be bought from a working strain, in which case a certificate of origin from champions has a real, practical value.

Before getting a dog, one should consider how much one is prepared to tax one's nerves. Very lively dogs like fox-terriers can easily upset a nervy person, particularly when their restlessness arises less from high spirits than from a too highly strung nervous system. When reflecting on the size of the dog in relation to one's house or flat, one should also take the temperament of the animal into consideration. A sentimental Setter, whose chief delight consists of gazing soulfully at his master, will suffer less from the confines of a town flat than will many a quicksilvery little terrier. Provided one can exercise the animal sufficiently, there is nothing to be said against keeping a large dog in the smallest flat. After all, one's dog demands no more than one's own health—half an hour's walk twice a day in good fresh air.

A mistake often made by animal lovers without much knowledge of dogs is to choose the one which makes the friendliest overtures on first acquaintance.

But one must not forget that one is thereby inevitably choosing the greatest fawner and that one will be less pleased later on when the dog greets every stranger in the same way. When I chose my Susi from a litter of nine yapping bundles of fur, I took her partly because her voice was raised the highest in indignation when I, the stranger, picked her up.

Sycophancy is one of the worst faults a dog can have and, as I have already mentioned, it comes from a persistence of the indiscriminate friendliness and servility which very young dogs show towards all people and adult dogs. It is a defect only in adult dogs; in young ones it is perfectly normal and in no way reprehensible. Unfortunately, it is impossible to foretell whether the playful young pup will grow into a sycophant or whether, with maturity, he will acquire the necessary aloofness towards strangers. Therefore, in the case of breeds which develop this restraint late, it is better not to buy a pup till he is five or six months old. This applies particularly to spaniels and other long-eared gun-dogs; Chows develop this exclusiveness early and even at eight or nine weeks of age they show marked individuality of character. If there is no danger of fawning, as in breeds which lack the predisposition, or when the prospective buyer is acquainted with both parents of the pup, I should advise him to get his dog as early as possible, that is, as soon as it can be removed from its mother with impunity. Of course the pup must still be given plenty of good food, particularly milk and meat, at frequent intervals; and an anti-rachitic medicine, such as cod-liver oil should be administered.

The younger the dog at the outset, the firmer generally becomes his attachment to his master in after life, and the more pleasure the latter will derive from his fully-grown dog when he recalls the effort it has cost him. Such recollections are worth a few chewed up shoes and one or two stains on the carpet.

A final piece of advice which arises from my own partiality and may therefore be taken or left by the reader: if possible get a bitch, even though her twice yearly season occasions a certain amount of inconvenience. I think that all knowledgeable dog-owners will agree with me in saying that a bitch is preferable to a dog in points of character. At one time, we had in our house in Altenberg four bitches, my Alsatian, Tito, my wife's Chow, Pygi, my brother's Dachshund, Kathi, and my sister-in-law's Bulldog bitch. My father owned the only dog, which had some difficulty in keeping unwelcome suitors off the premises. On

one occasion Pygi and Kathi were on heat at the same time, and as there was no danger of a misalliance—Pygi was absolutely faithful to our dog Bubi, and the diminutive Dachshund was too small to find a partner anywhere in the vicinity—these two were

allowed to accompany us to the Danube. I was quite
used to being followed by strange dogs but after we
had passed through the village this time, I was particularly struck by the size of our pack of followers
and I began to count: apart from our own five,
sixteen other dogs were running after us. All in all,
we had a canine escort of twenty-one! Nevertheless, I
repeat my counsel: a bitch is more faithful than a
dog, the intricacies of her mind are finer, richer and
more complex than his, and her intelligence is
generally greater. I have known very many dogs and
can say with firm conviction that of all creatures the
one nearest to man in the fineness of its perceptions
and in its capacity to render true friendship, is a
bitch. Strange that in English her name has become
a term of abuse.

9. AN APPEAL TO DOG BREEDERS

In Nature, there's no blemish but the mind.
SHAKESPEARE: *Twelfth Night*

CIRCUS dogs which can perform complicated tricks demanding great intelligence are very rarely equipped with a pedigree; this is not because the 'poor' artistes are unable to pay the price of a well bred dog—for fabulous fees are paid for talented circus dogs—but because it is mental rather than physical qualities that make good performing animals. It is not only their higher intelligence and better aptitude for learning which makes the mixed breeds of dogs more suitable for this work, but, above all, the fact that they are much less 'nervy', that is, their tougher constitution enables them to stand much more nervous strain. Of all the dogs that have been my constant companions, only one was fit for the show bench. This was an Alsatian, Bingo, who was certainly a noble creature, an aristocrat of unimpeachable character, but in fineness of feeling and sensitivity of soul not to be compared with my common or garden Alsatian bitch, Tito, who had no pedigree at all. My French Bulldog did have a pedigree but he was a throw-out and in no way embodied the ideals of pedigree dog breeding. He was far too big, his skull was far too long and so were his legs; his back was too straight; in short, he was, for a French Bulldog, a far too normal dog! But one thing I know: there was never a champion of this breed that could approach my Bully for mental qualities.

It is a sad but undeniable fact that breeding to a strict standard of physical points is incompatible with breeding for mental qualities. Individuals which conform to both sets of requirements are so rare that they would not even supply a foundation for the further propagation of their breed. Just as I am unable to think of any great intellectual who physically approaches anywhere near to an Adonis, or of a really beautiful woman who is even tolerably intelligent, in the same way I know of no 'champion' of any dog breed which I should ever wish to own myself. It is not that these two differently directed ideals are basically opposed to one another; it is hard to understand why a dog of perfect physique should not be endowed with equally desirable mental attributes—but each of the two ideals is, in itself, so rare that their combination in one and the same individual becomes a thing of the grossest improbability. Even a dog breeder who genuinely aspires to both ideals will find it well nigh impossible to achieve his aim without a compromise. In dog—as in pigeon-breeding, this compromise between two breeding ideals has been circumvented by separating 'show' and 'working' strains from each other. In pigeons it has already gone so far that show and 'working' carrier pigeons have become two distinct breeds of bird, and I think that of dogs the Alsatian is already well on the way to the same cleavage. Certainly some of the nervous and vicious show specimens which have earned a bad name for this breed in England have already evolved temperaments which deviate so far from the ideal as to put them in an entirely different

category from the genuine working Alsatians whose exceptional faculties enable them to serve man in countless different ways. In former times when the dog was more of a utility animal than it is to-day, mental qualities were unlikely to have been neg-~~lected when animals were chosen for stud. On the~~ other hand, however, character defects do appear in some types of dog which are used solely for working purposes, and a much respected authority on dogs is of the opinion that the lack of one-man fidelity in certain types of gun-dog is attributable to their vocation. Dogs of these breeds have been selected primarily for their fine sense of smell, and it is quite possible that animals lacking in single minded fidelity to one master were preferred: sportsmen and game-keepers often leave the search for wounded game to paid underlings and it is essential in a good gun-dog that he should work just as well with one of these as with his own master.

But the matter becomes serious when fashion, that silliest of all silly females, begins to dictate to the poor dog what he has got to look like, and there is no single breed of dog the originally excellent mental qualities of which have not been completely destroyed as a result of having become 'fashionable'. Only where, in some quiet corner of the world, the dog in question has gone on being bred for use and without any deference to fashion has such destruction been avoided. In their own home, there are still some strains of Scotch Collie in which the original excellent traits of the breed are extant, but the pedigree specimens, which first became popular all over Europe at the turn of the century, have been subjected to an almost incredible process of mental deterioration. In the same way, there are still true St Bernard dogs in the St Bernard monastery and in the admirable branch which its monks have established in Tibet, but in central Europe I have seen only degenerate mental cripples of this breed. Where breeding for use no longer provides the backbone for a breed undergoing 'modernization', the fate of that breed is sealed. Even those breeders who are idealists and would rather die than use a dog that fell short of the desired standard by one iota, do not consider it unethical to breed from physically beautiful but mentally defective dogs and to sell their offspring. Animal-loving reader, for whom I am writing this book, believe me in this: your pride that your dog conforms almost exactly to the ideal physical standards of his breed will dwindle with time but your annoyance at psychological defects, such as nervousness, viciousness, or excessive cowardice, will not. In fact, as time goes on, you will probably become increasingly aware of these nerve-wracking qualities, and in the long run you would certainly derive more pleasure from an intelligent, faithful and plucky nonpedigree dog than from your champion which probably cost you a fortune.

As I have already intimated, it would be quite possible for breeders to compromise in the choice of physical and mental properties, and this contention has been proved by the fact that various pure breeds of dog did retain their original good character traits until they fell a prey to fashion. Nevertheless dog shows in themselves involve certain dangers, since competition between pedigree dogs at shows must automatically lead to an exaggeration of all those points which characterize a breed. If one looks at old pictures which, in the case of English dog-breeds, can be found dating back to the middle ages, and compares them with pictures of present-day representatives of the same breeds, the latter look like evil caricatures of the original strain. In the Chow, which has only become really fashionable in the course of the last twenty years, this is particularly noticeable. In about 1920, Chows were still natural dogs, closely allied to the wild form, whose pointed muzzles, obliquely set Mongolian eyes and pricked ears pointing sharply upwards lent to their faces that fascinating expression which distinguishes Greenland sledge-dogs, Samoyeds and Huskies, in short all strongly wolf-blooded dogs. Modern breeding of the Chow has led to an exaggeration of those points which gives him the appearance of a plump bear: the muzzle is wide and short almost mastiff-like, the eyes have lost their slant in the compression of the whole face, and the ears have almost disappeared in the overgrown thickness of the coat. Mentally, too, these temperamental creatures, which still bore a trace of the wild beast of prey, have become stodgy teddy bears. But not my breed of Chows. These, flouting all the laws of dog-breeding societies, still contain some hundredth part of Alsatian blood.

Another breed of dog of which I am particularly fond and whose mental degeneration I similarly deplore is the Scottish Terrier. About thirty-five years ago, when my Scottish Terrier bitch, Ali, followed my footsteps, the dogs of this breed were, without exception, of exemplary courage and fidelity. None of my later dogs ever defended me so valorously as Ali, none did I so often save from hopeless fights with opponents of superior strength, from none did I so often have to save cats, and none of them but Ali ever followed a cat up a tree! She chased that cat up into the first fork of a somewhat slanting plum tree, shoulder-high above the ground. In the next instant, the cat was forced to retire another four feet higher up to the next fork, for Ali had scaled the trunk of the tree in one bound. Two seconds later, by landing on the thin bough the cat was sitting on she forced it to retreat further. Here, for a moment, Ali struggled to keep her hold before she dropped on to a lower branch which became wedged in her groin and so prevented her from falling altogether; thus she hung for a moment, head downwards. Then she slowly and painfully recovered her insecure stand in the fork and began to bark furiously at the cat which now sat scarcely three feet higher in the fragile upper branches. And now the incredible happened: Ali, tautening all her sinews for action, hurled herself up into the thin branches which stood no chance of bearing her weight. She could not keep her position but she could and did seize hold of the cat which for a few seconds hung on to the tree like grim death. Then they both crashed a good ten feet to the ground where I intervened on behalf of the cat, which Ali still had not released in spite of her heavy fall. The cat was uninjured but Ali limped for weeks as a result of torn muscles in her shoulder which had hit the ground first. Unlike cats, dogs do not always land dexterously on their feet.

Such were the Scotties of thirty-five years ago, for Ali was in no way an exception, and I am despondent when I see the behaviour of the present-day elegant and ebony-carved representatives of this breed in our dog-loving city of Vienna. I know that my tousled Ali, with one ear askew from a scar, would have stood no chance at a dog show beside these well-trimmed beauties. But they cringe before dogs which would have run shrieking from Ali.

There is still time. There are still Scotties which do not fear a St Bernard and which would fly at the legs of the strongest man who dared so much as a threatening word against their owners. But there are

only a few of this kind left and one will look for them in vain amongst the champions at a dog show. So I put a question to those breeders who are genuinely interested in the future of dogs: would it not be worth while to breed just for once from such a faithful and courageous dog even though, in the distribution of physical points, he fared much worse than those well-proportioned triumphs of modern hairdressing?

10. THE TRUCE

IT is remarkably easy to teach dogs, even confirmed hunters, that they must not touch other
animals kept in the same house. Even hard-bitten
cat-chasers, that cannot be curbed by severe punishment from pursuing a cat in the garden, not to
mention on the street, can quite easily be trained not
to do the same thing in the house, either to cats or
other animals. It has therefore become a habit of
mine to introduce any newly acquired animals to my
dogs within the four walls of my study. Why the dog
in the home is so much less bloodthirsty, I do not
know, but one thing is certain: that it is only his
hunting lust and not his fighting lust that is dimin-
ished in his own home. Every one of my dogs was
particularly aggressive towards any strange dog that
dared to enter our rooms. I have never had the
opportunity of observing the same thing in other
dogs, because on principle I never take my own dogs
into the homes of other people who keep dogs. That
is simple consideration for others, not only because a
dog fight gets on most people's nerves—it does not
worry me personally because my dogs usually win—
but because the visit of a strange member of his own
species releases in the average male dog a response

which is not welcome to every house-wife. The leg-lifting of a dog has a very definite meaning which is, paradoxically, exactly the same as that of a nightingale's song: it means the marking of the territory, warning off all intruders by telling them as clearly as their senses can perceive it that they are trespassing on the ground owned by somebody else. Nearly all mammals mark their territory by means of scent, as being one of their strongest sense faculties. A well-trained dog will abstain from this 'marking of territory' in his own home—since the atmosphere is in any case sufficiently pervaded by his own smell or that of his human owners. But if a strange dog, or worse still a well-known and detested enemy, should once cross the threshold, however fleetingly, then these inhibitions are at once dispelled. In this case, every more or less lusty dog considers it his bounden duty to dispel the odour of his enemy by applying a concentrated trade-mark of his own. To the disgust of the owner, particularly if it is a woman, this clean house-trained dog goes round the whole building lifting his leg, shamelessly against one piece of furniture after another. Think of this ere you enter a dog-owner's house with your own dog!

This pacifism of the dog in his own home thus holds good only for potential prey and not for his own kind. It is possible that we have here an age-old and, in the animal kingdom, very widespread behaviour reaction, or, better expressed, inhibition. It is well-known that hawks and many other birds of prey do not hunt in the near vicinity of their eyrie. Wood-pigeon nests with fully grown young have been found in the immediate precincts of hawk's eyries, and there exists reliable information that sheldrake have nested and hatched their young in inhabited fox earths. It is also reported of the wolf that it allows young roe-deer to grow up unmolested in the immediate neighbourhood of its den. I think it possible that it is just this age-old law of 'cease-fire' that makes our house-dog so peaceable in his home towards animals of so many different kinds.

This inhibition against killing prey in the home is no absolute one, and strong measures are required to teach a vigorous young dog with a keen appetite for hunting that the cat, badger, wild rabbit, mouse or other animal with which, from now on, he will have to share his master, not only must not be eaten but is untouchable, sacred, in other words, completely tabu! I remember as clearly as if it were yesterday how, many years ago, I brought home my first kitten—it was Thomas I—and tried to impress upon my dog, Bully, one of the keenest of cat-hunters, that he must leave the little thing alone. As I unpacked the tiny kitten, Bully rushed up expectantly, giving vent to his seldom heard but very personal deep, howling whine, and wagging his stump of a tail so fast that you could hardly see it, being, of course, firmly convinced that I had produced the cat for the sole purpose of giving him the fun of shaking it to death. This belief was perhaps not unjustified since I had, on numerous previous occasions, presented him with old teddy bears, stuffed dogs etc. for the same purpose, his droll antics with such sham prey being so highly entertaining. But now, to his intense disappointment, I made it quite clear to him that this kitten was tabu. Bully was an uncommonly good-natured and obedient dog, and I had little fear that he would ignore my command and molest the kitten. I therefore did not interfere as he approached it carefully and smelt it all over, although at the same time his whole body quivered with agitation and his smooth, glossy coat betrayed, in the region of neck and shoulders, that ominous dull black patch which took the place of a ruffled mane.

Bully did nothing to the cat but from time to time he looked round at me, whimpered in his deep bass, wagged his tail like an electric fan and danced up and down, marking time with all four feet. This was his way of appealing to me to start at last the longed-for game of chasing and shaking to death this grand new toy. But as I merely continued, with increasing emphasis and uplifted forefinger, to repeat the word, 'No-o-o-o', he gave me a look as though he doubted my sanity, threw a last, contemptuously uninterested glance at the kitten, dropped his ears, and, heaving a deep sigh as only a French bulldog can, sprang on the sofa and curled himself up. From that moment he ignored the kitten completely, and on the very same day I left him for hours alone with it knowing that I could rely on my dog. It was not that his longing to shake the animal had been so quickly allayed; on the contrary, every time I turned my attention to it, particularly when I picked it up, his apathy fell from Bully like a cloak and he rushed up, wagging his tail wildly and trampling excitedly with all four feet till the ground shook. At the same time, he watched me with the same tense and happily expectant expression which lit up his face when he was very hungry and I entered the room with a bowl of food still too hot to eat.

I was, at this time, still very young; nevertheless, I was struck by the innocent look on the face of the dog, all of whose senses were quick with longing to tear the tiny kitten to pieces. I was already quite familiar with the physiognomy of an angry dog; only too well did I know the expressive movements with which he demonstrated his hate; but I now realized for the first time a fact which simultaneously pained and consoled me, namely that the act of killing in a beast of prey is entirely free from hatred. It is self-evident and yet paradoxical that the beast of prey bears no more resentment towards the animal it intends to kill than I do towards the boiled ham which I intend to eat for supper and whose delicious odour emanating from the kitchen presages a pleasant evening. The prey is not a 'friend' of the killer. If you could convince the lion that the hunted gazelle were his sister, or the fox that the rabbit were his brother, they would no doubt be just as astonished as a man whom you informed that Man was his bitterest enemy. Only those beings which do not know that their prey is one of themselves can kill without incurring blame, and it is this blamelessness that man seeks vainly to regain when he tries to forget that the object of his slaughter is an animated being like himself, or when he deceives himself into believing that his adversary is a veritable fiend, less worthy of compassion than a mad dog.

In one of his Arctic novels, Jack London describes with ghastly realism, the 'innocent face of greed' of the beast of prey. The hero, who has fired his last cartridge, is pressed close by a large pack of wolves which gains courage and ferocity as his helplessness increases. Finally, overcome by exhaustion and lack of sleep, he dozes off by the side of his dying fire. Fortunately he awakens in a few minutes to see that the circle of wolves has closed in still further. Now he obtains a full view of their faces and notices that the brutal, threatening expression has left them altogether; no more wrinkled noses, cruel slit-eyes, bared fangs or wickedly flattened ears; no more growling, only a deep silence and a circle of friendly-looking, anticipatory dog faces with pricked ears and widely opened eyes. Only when one wolf shifts impatiently from one foot to the other, at the same time drawing his tongue over his lips, does the man realize with horror the blood-curdling significance of these friendly countenances: the wolves have so far lost their fear of him as to see in him no longer a ~~dangerous enemy but only an appetizing meal.~~ I am quite sure that if somebody should photograph me, from the 'point of view' of the above mentioned boiled ham my features too would present an entirely benevolent expression.

Even after many weeks, the slightest sign from me would have sufficed for the bulldog to kill the cat. But this permission not being given, he not only left it severely alone but also defended it manfully against other dogs. This was not because he liked it but probably because he took the view 'If I am not allowed to kill this wretched cat in my own house, then certainly no other dog is going to!'

From the very beginning, the kitten never showed the slightest fear of Bully—certainly a sign that the cat has no instinctive understanding of the facial expressions of the dog. I, or any other being familiar with them, would have been frightened to death by those glances of ill-restrained greed, but not so the kitten: unconscious of the risk, it continually attempted to play, either making amiable passes at him, or what was much more dangerous, provoking him into chasing it. This it did by approaching him coaxingly and then suddenly taking flight in the hopes that he would follow. At such moments as these my good little Bully needed all his powers of self-control, and shivers of incipient passion would traverse his muscular frame. I am perfectly certain that, without previous experience, cats do not understand the expressive movements of dogs although they are so similar to their own. Cats which are on friendly terms with dogs in the same house display a trust-fulness towards strange dogs which may, and sometimes does, lead to their own ruin. I have often observed how such a cat will stare with fearless innocence full into the eyes of a strange dog which is bracing itself unequivocally for attack. It is equally unusual for a cat-friendly dog to understand the threatening of an angry cat, unless it has already learnt to do so by bitter experience. This is quite re-markable, for one would surely expect the growling of the cat to be intelligible to the dog, which expresses its emotion in just the same way.

I once took my then seven months old Chow bitch, Susi, to visit the owners of a large Persian cat, which received her with arched back and ominous growls. Susi, nothing daunted, approached with wagging tail and inquisitively pricked ears, stretching her nose tentatively towards it as she would have done to any friendly dog. Even when she had received the first cuff from the cat's paw, she still apparently imagined there was some mistake, for she continued with her friendly advances; nor did a sound box on her silver-grey nose offend her seriously: she merely sneezed, wiped her nose with her fat puppy paw, and turned disdainfully away from her inhospitable feline hostess.

After some weeks, Bully's attitude towards the cat underwent a change: I do not know whether this alteration in his feelings was sudden or whether a friendship between the animals had gradually matured in my absence. One day I noticed how Thomas once more coyly approached the dog and again abruptly turned tail. To my horrified astonish-ment, the dog leapt up and rushed furiously after the kitten which disappeared behind the sofa. With his large head wedged firmly beneath this piece of furni-ture the dog remained lying, only responding to my

flabbergasted expostulations by ardent waggings of
his short stump. This did not necessarily signify a
friendly disposition towards the cat, since he would
also vehemently wag his tail when his teeth were
embedded in the flesh of a hated enemy. In front he
would bite with murderous intent whilst behind he
was wagging most amiably. What an extraordinarily
complicated mechanism of the brain. Obviously the
posterior activities were thus to be interpreted: 'Dear
Master, please do not be cross but, for the moment,
I much regret to say, I am quite unable to let go of
this dirty dog, even if you should think fit to punish
me later by a whacking or—as God forbid—at this
instant with a bucket of cold water.' But this was
not the kind of wagging that Bully was indulging in
just then. A moment later as, obedient to my call,
Bully was extricating himself from the sofa, Thomas
shot out like a cannon-ball, precipitated himself upon him, dug one set of claws into his neck,
the other into his face and, painstakingly twisting his
little face upwards from below, attempted to bite him
in the gullet. For one moment I had before me on
the carpet a wonderfully plastic group, resembling to
the last detail a picture by the famous animal painter,
Wilhelm Kuhnert, who has portrayed a lion killing
a buffalo with just the same artistic movements.

Bully at once played up, most convincingly mim-
icking the movements of the victimized buffalo. He
collapsed heavily in front, yielding to the drag of the
tiny paws, and rolled over on to his back emitting as
he did so a most realistic death-rattle, such as only a
happy bulldog or an expiring buffalo can ever produce. When he had had enough of being slaughtered,
Bully took the initiative and, jumping up, shook the
kitten off. The latter fled but after a few yards
allowed itself to be overtaken by turning the kind of

somersault I shall describe later on. And now, for the first time in my life, I watched one of the most delightful animal games that one can ever witness. The contrast in conformation and movement between the fat, black, shiny muscular body of the dog, and the supple grey-striped feline form, so tiger-like in its markings and movements, presented a fascinating spectacle. An interesting scientific point about such games of cats with playmates larger than themselves lies in the fact that this particular set of movements is concerned with killing prey and has nothing to do with fighting. From what I have seen of both sham and real fights in cats, I believe that these movements are never executed in battle. A prey into whose neck the attacker digs its claws, biting into its gullet from below, must necessarily be larger than the predator, but neither our domestic cat nor its wild progenitor is accustomed to killing prey of this size; thus this highly interesting and certainly not rare phenomenon is probably attributable to the fact that a genealogically ancient set of movements, which is widely distributed in related groups of animals has, in the groups of which we are speaking, lost its original function for the preservation of the species. It has, however, retained its hereditary character though it is now only manifested in play.

After the death of Thomas I, it was many years before I was again able to watch a cat performing 'buffalo-killing movements' in play. This time the 'lion' was a large silver-tabby tom-cat, a close friend of my one and a half year old daughter, Dagmar. The cat, which was temperamental and anything but placid, would put up with a lot from the child, letting her carry him round continually although he was nearly as large as herself and his beautiful black and silver ringed tail always trailed along the ground

where, sooner or later, it was trodden on by Dagmar who promptly stumbled over it and fell on him. It was certainly to his credit that even then he still did not bite or scratch. However he exacted reprisals by requiring Dagmar to act as buffalo and it was thrilling to watch him ambush her, then pounce on her, clutching her tightly and fastening his teeth into some part of her body. But of course it was never in earnest. The child would then yell but likewise never in earnest. My theory that these movements are a relic of former hunting habits is further corroborated by the fact that they are thus preceded in play by a highly realistic lying-in-wait and stalking process.

Bully and Thomas rejoiced in a friendship which far surpassed the mutual tolerance commonly shown by dogs and cats which inhabit the same house, and their affection proved its stability on the occasions when they met out of doors. They then greeted each other, the cat with the lip sounds I have described and the dog with a friendly tail-wag. It does not necessarily follow that dogs which are friendly to cats in the house will be the same outside. In my room, our present dogs have no objections to our somewhat lethargic cat, and indeed Susi plays with her quite charmingly, nor does the cat show any fear of the dogs and even steals their food and plays 'mouse' with the tips of their tails—she is not vivacious enough for the buffalo-killing game. In other rooms, however, she is much more wary and generally avoids the dogs, at the most tantalizing them from beneath a low piece of furniture or from the top of a high one, but she carefully avoids being chased. Out of doors, her conduct again alters: she evinces definite fear of the dogs and quite justifiably, for Wolfi shows unmistakable signs of wanting a cat hunt. Even more strained were the relations between Stasi and

Dagmar's wild silver-tabby tom-cat. In the house, she ignored him completely but outside she hunted him so assiduously that when one day he disappeared altogether, I rather had my suspicions of Stasi.

The difficulty of placing under control his strong desires to hunt different animals with whom he may be obliged to share a house varies in the dog according to the species of animal with which he is confronted. It is quite easy to teach even the most inveterate hunter not to kill tame birds, as we see in 'Beau's reply' to his master Cowper,

> *And when your linnet on a day,*
> *Passing his prison door,*
> *Had fluttered all his strength away,*
> *And panting pressed the floor,*
> *Well knowing him a sacred thing,*
> *Not destined to my tooth,*
> *I only kissed his ruffled wing,*
> *And lick'd the feathers smooth.*

But to impart the same feeling for various small mammals is extremely difficult. The most seductive of all small game seems to be the rabbit, and even dogs which are perfectly 'cat-trained' are not always to be relied upon with these. My own dogs are just the same, and Susi who, inconceivably, shows no interest in golden hamsters, makes no attempt to conceal her craving for the delightful little Jerboa, which leaps freely about my room and which she is under the strictest orders not to touch. Many years ago I had a great surprise when I brought home a tame young badger and introduced it to the savage Alsatians which I kept at that time. I fully expected that this strange, wild creature would release all the worst hunting instincts in my dogs, but exactly the opposite was the case: the badger, which had

formerly lived in the house of a forester and had obviously been accustomed to dogs, approached them
fearlessly, and the dogs, though they certainly sniffed
it with an unwonted caution and reserve, made it
clear from the first that they did not regard it as game
but as a somewhat unusual member of their own
kind. A few hours later they were playing with it in
unrestrained intimacy, and it was interesting to observe how the antics of this tough-hided newcomer
were obviously too rough for his thinner-skinned
playmates who now and then let out a yelp of pain.
Even so the game never degenerated into a fight. From
the first the dogs put all their trust in the social inhibitions of the badger and allowed him to roll them
on their backs, seize them by the throat, and, according to all the rules of the game, to 'throttle' them,
just as they would have allowed a friendly dog to do.

The behaviour of all my dogs towards monkeys
was peculiar. To begin with, I had to subject them
to the strictest regulations in order to protect my
lemurs, particularly the very attractive little Maxi,
whom even later the dogs were inclined to hunt if
they came upon her in the garden. This, however,
only seemed to amuse her, nor were they entirely
to blame, for Maxi's favourite joke was to steal up
from behind, tweak one of the dogs in the rump or
pull its tail and then swing herself up into a tree,
where, from a safe height, she dangled her tail just out
of reach of the infuriated dogs. Still more equivocal
were Maxi's relations with the cats, particularly with
Bussy, the mother of countless litters of kittens. Maxi
was a spinster and, although I had twice got a husband for her, she had never managed to get married.
Her first mate went blind shortly after I got him and
the second one met with an accident. So Maxi
remained childless and, like many other childless
females, envied happy mothers their family blessing;

while Bussy was blessed at least twice a year. Maxi evolved just such a tender affection for the kittens as my mother's unmarried sister had for our children, but whereas my wife often gratefully submitted our children to the care of my good Aunt Hedwig, Bussy had different ideas. She was exceedingly mistrustful of the lemur who, if she wanted a kitten to 'love and kiss', had to adopt a special strategy in order to obtain her end, and she usually succeeded. No matter how carefully the mother hid her litter or how vigilantly she watched over them, Maxi managed somehow to find them and, creeping up stealthily from behind, to abduct one of the kittens; she never wanted more than one. She held the kidnapped baby just as a lemur mother holds its young, pressing it against her belly with one hind foot. With her remaining three legs she could still run faster and climb better than the cat, even if it caught her red-handed and raced straight after her. The hunt usually ended in a tree where the lemur settled down in the topmost fragile boughs, which were inaccessible to the cat, and where she proceeded to indulge in a veritable orgy of child-nursing. The innate, instinctive movements of cleaning were the most important part of the ceremony, and Maxi diligently combed the kitten, which quite enjoyed the process, all over, paying special attention to those parts of the body which, in all babies, are deserving of particular care. Of course we always did our best to remove the kitten as soon as possible, for we were afraid that Maxi might one day let it fall through the branches, but this, in fact, never happened.

There was an interesting question that I found difficult to answer: how did Maxi recognize the kitten as a 'baby'? It had nothing to do with size, for she showed not the slightest interest in adult mammals of approximately the same dimensions, but when later

on my bitch Tito—a contemporary of Maxi—produced a litter, the devoted 'aunt' showed exactly the
same feeling or the puppies as previously for the
kittens, nor did her love abate when the rapidly
growing puppies had reached more than twice her
own size. At my insistence Tito rather unwillingly
allowed Maxi to work off her repressed brood-tending instincts on the litter of puppies. This led to the
drollest scenes and the most delightful games between the lemur and the young dogs. When my
eldest son Thomas was born, Maxi welcomed him as
a most satisfying object of care and would sit beside
him in the pram for hours on end. To people un-
accustomed to the sight of lemurs this presented
rather an uncanny spectacle, for there is no doubt
that one requires an insight into the weird physiognomy of these animals in order to appreciate how
sweet-tempered and attractive they really are. To
the uninitiated the head is almost ghostly with its
black face, its protruding 'human' ears, its pointed
nose, its slightly projecting canine teeth, and above
all its enormous amber-yellow nocturnal eyes whose
pupils are contracted by day to a tiny, piercing pin-
point. The old zoologists referred to this group of
animals as 'the ghostly lemurs'. But one could as
safely entrust the child to the care of this animal as
to that of my aunt. It was every bit as certain that
the lemur would do it no harm; but for that very
reason the love of the little creature for the child led
to a tragic conflict: her jealousy made her so
aggressive towards its rightful nurses that she could
no longer be allowed to run about loose. I was the
only person whom she allowed to approach the child
when she happened to be 'looking after' it.

Entirely different from their treatment of the lemur
was the behaviour of my dogs and cats towards real
monkeys, irrespective of whether these were the

minute marmoset or our hooded capuchin, Gloria,
which was rather larger than a cat.

It is a widely spread belief that there is a strange
power in the eyes of man. Mowgli was expelled from
the wolf pack because they could not bear his gaze,
and even his best friend the panther was unable to
look him straight in the eyes. As in many, though
certainly not all superstitions, there is also an element
of truth in this one. It is certainly characteristic of
birds and mammals that they do not look at each
other, or at a trusted human being, directly; that is,
they do not fix them with their gaze. Very few animals possess that specialization of the retina which
enables man to see a sharply defined picture. In man
the central groove of the retina is specialized for clear
seeing, the outer segments of this membrane rendering a less clear cut picture, and for this reason our
eyes wander constantly from one point to the next,
focusing each one in turn on to the middle part (*fovea
centralis*). It is an illusion that we receive an impression of the whole picture at once as in a photograph. In nearly all animals there is a much less
definite division of function between the centre and
the periphery of the retina than in man, that is, they
see less clearly with the former and more clearly with
the latter.

For this reason, most animals fix their gaze much
less often and for much shorter periods than man.
Take a cross-country walk with a dog and notice how
often he looks at you directly. You will find out that
in the course of hours this happens but once or twice,
and it seems almost as a coincidence that he is taking
the same path as yourself. This is explained by the
fact that he can quite easily locate his master by
peripheral vision. Most of those animals which are
able to fix their eyes binocularly, as fishes, reptiles,
birds and mammals, only do so in moments of utmost

stress when they have a certain object in view; but man is continuously focusing one point after another on the central groove of the retina, so that it strikes us at once as odd if for a moment he omits to do so and 'gazes into space'. In the overwhelming majority of animals this empty gazing is the normal state of affairs. If an animal fixes his eyes carefully and for a long time on some part of its surroundings it means unequivocally that he is either afraid of it or that he has some special purport with it, and usually no good one. The fixation of the eyes in such an animal is almost equivalent to taking aim. If I try to find concrete examples of the cases when my dog thus regards me I am, even after long consideration, only able to cite three, firstly when I enter the room with his food bowl, secondly in mock fights, and thirdly—and then only for a moment—when I call him sharply. Amongst themselves, animals only look at each other fixedly when they intend to take drastic measures or are afraid of each other. Consequently they conceive a prolonged fixed gaze as being something hostile and threatening and rate it in man as the expression of extreme malevolence. And this is the whole secret of the 'power of the human eye'. If I were suddenly to find myself, without any interposing bars, in the company of a large beast of prey whose feelings towards myself were as yet uncertain, and if this beast were to fix its wide-eyed gaze constantly upon me—just as man does in everyday contacts with his fellow beings—then, I admit, I should make myself scarce as quickly as possible. In this case, the 'power of the lion's eye' would certainly be quite considerable. Corresponding with the difference in the physiology of their vision, the direct glance denotes almost the opposite in man from that which it signifies in the canine or feline beast of prey. The man who cannot look me straight in the eyes but constantly looks from one side of me to the other either has evil intentions or he is afraid of me—embarrassment is only a mild form of fear. The same precept holds good for the animal which feels itself bound to keep me constantly under its scrutiny. On all these observations, we can found a code of manners for our own dealings with animals: anyone who wishes to win the confidence of a shy cat, a nervous dog, or any other similar being, should make it a rule never to face him and stare straight at him like a hungry lion, but to look beyond him, only letting the eye rest on him, as it were by accident and for a very short time.

Now the physiology of the eye of true monkeys is exactly similar to that of man; in them too the eyes are so placed in the skull as to face directly forwards, with the same function of focusing surrounding objects. Since monkeys are insatiably curious and employ no tact or diplomacy in their dealings with other creatures, they jar horribly on the nerves of other higher mammals, particularly dogs and cats. The way these animals react to monkeys is a fair reflection of their attitude towards man. Dogs which are gentle and submissive towards man allow themselves to be completely tyrannized even by the tiniest of little apes. I have never had to protect capuchin monkeys from even the strongest and most savage dogs; on the contrary, I have often had to interfere on the side of the dog. My little white-headed capuchin monkey, Emil, who undoubtedly loved Bully in his own way, made use of him alternately as a horse and a hot water bottle. But if the dog offered the slightest resistance to the will of this forward little creature, he was immediately castigated with cuffs and bites. He was not allowed to rise from his place on the sofa while Emil needed him as a warming pan, and I was always obliged to remove Emil at feeding time, otherwise he worried the unfortunate dog persistently although he would never have dreamed of actually eating the frugal canine fare. On the whole, dogs behave towards monkeys as they do towards spoilt and ill-natured children who, as is well known, can tease good-tempered dogs with impunity and without receiving in return one well-deserved bite or even so much as an angry growl.

My remarks about the way dogs behave with children apply to a large extent also to my cats. Cats, however, are not quite so long-suffering with children, though they are certainly much more patient with them than with grown-ups. As for monkeys, Thomas I never hesitated with growls and hisses, to give Maxi a good sound box on the ears, when she pulled his tail, and my other cats were equally capable of holding their own with the monkeys. They probably benefited by the fact that, according to my observations, monkeys have a certain innate fear of feline beasts of prey. My two marmosets, which were born in captivity and therefore could not possibly have had any alarming experience with such animals, were utterly terrified of a stuffed tiger in the Zoological Institute and were always extremely cautious of our house cats. My capuchin monkey, also, showed in the beginning much more respect for the cats than for the dogs, though the former were certainly much smaller.

I do not like sentimental anthropomorphization of animals. It makes me feel slightly sick when, in some magazine published by an animal defence society, I read the caption 'Good Friends' or something of the kind under a picture which portrays a cat, a dachshund and a robin all eating out of the same dish, or worse, as I recently saw, a Siamese cat and a little alligator sitting like two complete strangers next to each other. From my own experience, I should say that real friendships between members of different species only exist between man and animals, and hardly ever between animals amongst themselves, and it is for this reason that I have called this chapter, 'The Truce' and not 'Animal Friendships' or anything like that. Mutual toleration is certainly not synonymous with friendship, and even when animals unite in a common interest, as for a game, it cannot generally be said that they are bound by a real social contact, far less by a firm friendship. My raven, Roah, who used to fly miles to find me on some Danube sand-bank, my grey-lag goose Martina who, the longer I had been away, the more enthusiastically she greeted me, my wild ganders Peter and Victor who would defend me valiantly against the attacks of a wicked old gander of whom they themselves were mortally afraid, all these animals were really my friends, that is to say our love was mutual. The fact that corresponding feelings seldom occur in animals of different species is largely due to the 'language difficulty'. I have already mentioned the difficulties that arise between dogs and cats, because neither has an innate understanding of even the most significant expressive movement of threat or anger made by the other; much less can they apprehend all the finer lights and shades of the emotion of friendship which both are capable of feeling and showing. Even the relationship between Bully and Thomas I, which, through the increase of mutual understanding and the power of familiarity, certainly reached a certain depth, could hardly be called friendship, and the same applies to my Alsatian, Tito, and the badger. These two relationships were the most intimate and the nearest approach to real friendship that I ever saw between animals of different species in my house; and, in the course of the years, very many and very different species have lived there in a

state of armistice and with every opportunity to form heartfelt friendships.

I do know one case, of which I was an eye witness, of a real bond between a dog and cat, and this concerned a chequered mongrel and a tri-coloured female cat which lived in a farm-house in our village. The dog was rather weak and cowardly, the cat was exactly the opposite, but was much the older of the two, and had apparently developed something akin to maternal feelings for the dog in the days when he was still a puppy. On this foundation was built up the closest friendship between a dog and a cat that I have ever had occasion to witness. The two animals not only played together but had a marked preference for each other's company and they would do something I have never seen anywhere else: they would go for walks together in the garden or even down the village street. This extraordinary animal union even stood up to friendship's ultimate test: the dog was one of the recognized enemies of my French bulldog, chiefly because he was one of the few members of his race who was smaller than Bully and who held him in any awe. One day, Bully surprised the little mongrel on the village street and involved him in a serious scrap. Believe it or not, the tri-coloured cat shot through the door of the house and across the garden right into the middle of the street, darted like a fury into the fray, put Bully to flight in the space of a few seconds, and rode him, like a witch on a broomstick for a considerable stretch down the road away from the scene of action! If such an undertaking is possible, one has still less right to speak of 'friendship' when an overfed, phlegmatic town dog and a cat of the same ilk eat from one dish without doing each other any damage.

11. THE FENCE

AN everyday occurrence: you are walking along
the front of a garden fence and a big dog is
growling and barking behind it. Judging by the
behaviour of the animal, which is snarling and biting
the fence with brutally bared fangs, it is only the
railings that keep him from your throat. On such
occasions I am not intimidated by these threats of
violence and I always open the garden gate without
hesitation. The dog demurs; unsure of what to do
next, he continues to bark but in much less menacing
tones, and his demeanour plainly betrays that he
would never have exhibited so much fury had he
foreseen that I would not respect the inviolability of
the fence. It may even happen that when the gate is
opened, he flees several yards and then keeps up his
barking in a different tone and from a safe distance.
And conversely a very shy dog, or wolf, which shows
no sign of enmity or mistrust from behind the bars,
may attack in deadly earnest anyone appearing in
the doorway.

These apparently opposite types of behaviour can
all be explained in terms of the same psychological
mechanism. Every animal, particularly every large
mammal, will flee before a superior rival as soon as
it comes within a certain fixed distance. The 'flight
distance', as Prof. Hediger, its discoverer, calls it,

increases proportionately with the degree of fear which the animal possesses for its opponent. There is an exactly predictable point at which an animal will turn tail when an enemy starts to encroach on the flight distance, and there is a similar point at which it will fight if the enemy gets very close. Under natural conditions, such an overstepping of the 'critical distance' (Hediger) only occurs in two instances, either when the animal is taken by surprise or when it is cornered and so unable to flee. A variation of the first possibility takes place when a large animal capable of aggression sees its opponent approaching and reacts not by flight but by taking cover, in the hope that the enemy will pass by without seeing it. If, however, the concealed animal is discovered by its enemy it will put up a desperate fight. It is this mechanism which makes the search for wounded big game so uncommonly dangerous. The attack on an aggressor that oversteps the critical distance is reinforced by all the courage of abandonment and despair, and is far the most dangerous struggle which the animal in question can ever wage. This type of reaction is not peculiar to the large predatory animals but is well marked in our indigenous hamster; while the furious attack of a rat in a corner from which there is no escape has given rise to the saying, 'fighting like a cornered rat'.

The effects of the flight distance and the critical distance help to explain the behaviour of the dog behind the closed and open garden gates. The dividing fence is equivalent to a separating distance of many yards; the animal behind it feels safe and is correspondingly brave. The opening of the door gives the animal the feeling that the foe has suddenly approached that amount nearer. It may have dangerous consequences for the uninitiated, par-

ticularly with zoo animals that have been in captivity a long time and are convinced of the impregnability of their cages. With the fence between itself and a man, the creature feels safe, its flight distance not being encroached on. It will even indulge in a friendly social contact with the human being on the other side of the bars. But should the man, relying on the fact that the animal has just allowed itself to be stroked through the railings, step unexpectedly into the cage, it may flee in terror but it may actually attack, since the flight distance and also the much smaller critical distance have both become breached with the removal of the barrier. The animal will of course be branded as 'treacherous'.

I ascribe the fact that I was not attacked by a tame wolf to my previous knowledge of these laws. As I have already related, I once wished to mate my bitch, Stasi, with a big Siberian wolf at the Königsberg Zoo, an undertaking which I was strongly advised against, as it had a ferocious reputation. However I decided to risk it and took the precaution of first putting the two animals in adjacent cages of the reserve department. I opened the communicating door just wide enough for Stasi and the wolf to stick their noses through it and sniff each other. After this ⌣eremony they both wagged their tails, and a few minutes later I pushed the door right open, a deed which I never regretted for there was never any friction between the two from that moment onwards.

When I saw my friend Stasi playing amicably with the enormous grey wolf I suddenly felt an urge to try my skill as a wild-beast tamer and likewise to visit the wolf in his lair. Since he treated me through the bars with great friendliness, such a step would appear to the uninitiated to be quite devoid of risk. Nevertheless it would have been a dangerous enterprise,

had I been ignorant of the relationship between cage
bars and critical distance. I coaxed Stasi and the
wolf into the furthest of the long row of cages, having
first evacuated a few dogs, a jackal and a hyaena for
the purpose. Then I opened all the connecting doors
and walked slowly and carefully into the first cage,
stopping at a point where I could see straight through
all the cages. The animals did not notice me at first,
for they were standing out of the direct line of communicating doors, but after a little while the wolf
glanced through the last door and saw me; and the
same wolf which knew me so well, which had licked
my hands through the bars and let me scratch its
head, which greeted me with joyful bounds when he
saw me coming, was frightened to death at the sight
of me, standing a few yards away without any intervening bars. His ears fell, his mane bristled threateningly, and, with his tail tucked tightly between his
legs, he disappeared from the doorway like a streak
of lightning. The next moment he returned still looking scared but no longer bristling, and, holding his
head a little on one side, he watched me closely; then
his tail began to wag in little short strokes from between his legs. I looked tactfully to one side, for a
fixed gaze frightens animals whose equanimity is
disturbed. At this juncture, Stasi too discovered me.
Squinting along the line of doors, I saw her rushing
towards me at a gallop, closely followed by—the
wolf. I will admit that for a fraction of a second I was
horribly afraid, but I instantly recovered my
equanimity on seeing the wolf approach me in a
clumsily playful canter and just a hint of that head-
shaking which, as all observant dog-lovers know, is
an invitation to play. So I braced all my muscles to
receive the friendly impact of the colossal beast,
standing sideways to avoid the notorious, terrible

kick in the belly. In spite of these precautions I was flung crashing against the wall. But the wolf was again trustful and friendly. One can only realize the enormous force and roughness of his play by imagining a dog with the sinews of a fox-terrier and the strength of a Great Dane, and during this game it became quite clear to me why a wolf is often more than a match for a whole pack of dogs, for in spite of my most careful foot-work I continually landed on the floor.

Another fence story concerns my old Bully and his mortal enemy, a white Spitz, which lived in a house whose long, narrow garden flanked the village street and was bordered by green wooden railings. Along the thirty yards of this fence the two heroes would gallop backwards and forwards, barking furiously and only stopping for a moment at the turning points at both ends in order to curse each other with all the gestures and sounds of frustrated fury. One day, an embarrassing situation arose: the fence was undergoing repairs and parts of it had been carried away for the purpose. The upper fifteen yards of the fence, that is, the part furthest from the Danube, still remained, while the lower half was gone. Now Bully and I came down the hill from our house, on our way to the river. The Spitz of course, had noticed us and was waiting growling and quivering with excitement at the topmost corner of the garden. First of all, a stationary cursing duel took place as usual, then the dogs, one each side of the fence, broke into their customary gallop along its front. And now the disaster happened: they ran past the place where the fence had been removed and only noticed their error on their arrival at the lower corner of the garden, where a further cursing match was due. There they stood with bristling hair and brutally

bared fangs and—there was no fence. Immediately their barking ceased. And now, what did they do? As one dog, they turned about and rushed flank to flank back to the still remaining fence where they recommenced their barking as though nothing had happened.

12. MUCH ADO ABOUT A LITTLE DINGO

ONE cloudy day in the year 1939, my friend Prof. Antonius, the Director of the Schönbrunn Zoo, rang me up: 'You said you wanted a young Dingo for your bitch to rear. My Dingo bitch pupped six days ago; if you come straight over you can choose him yourself—right, I'll expect you in half an hour.'

On hearing this exciting news I rushed straight for the Underground, quite forgetting that I had another important engagement for that morning. Arrived at Schönbrunn, I enticed the tame, good-natured Dingo mother into another compartment of the cage and picked out a dog pup from amongst the red-brown bundles that were crawling about the whelping box; I chose the only one that had none of those white markings which signify the former dependence of his ancestors on man.

The Dingo is a remarkable animal: it is the only larger mammal—not belonging to the sub-class of marsupials—that was found when the continent of Australia was discovered. Apart from these, the only representatives of the higher mammals were a few bats which had found their way to Australia. Otherwise the whole mammal fauna of this continent, which had obviously been isolated geographically for a very long time, consisted exclusively of marsupials,

a type of mammal with many primitive characteristics. The only other non marsupial mammals of
Australia were the black Aboriginals, a people of
extraordinarily low cultural standing, with no experience of agriculture or domestic animals, and who
were on a much lower mental and cultural plane
than their ancestors, the first settlers, must have been.
The latter were doubtlessly a sea-faring people just
as the people of New Guinea are to-day.

The loss of culture amongst the Aboriginals is
probably connected with the ease with which they
could feed themselves: many marsupials being stupid
and easily caught.

The question has been much debated, whether the
Dingo is a true wild dog or whether it was originally
a domestic dog brought to Australia by the first
settlers who reached the continent. I am quite convinced that the latter theory is the correct one. Nobody who is acquainted with the markings of
domesticity can doubt for a minute that the Dingo is
a secondary wild domestic animal. Brehm's contention that its gait is that of a 'true wild dog such
as is never seen in the domestic dog' is quite wrong:
every Eskimo or Husky shows more resemblance in
its movements to the wolf or jackal than the Dingo
does. Added to this is the fact that the pure-blooded
Dingo often has white 'stockings' or stars and nearly
always a white tip to its tail, these points being quite
irregularly distributed, a feature never seen in wild
animals but of frequent occurrence in all domestic
breeds. I myself have no doubt whatever that it was
man who brought the Dingo to Australia and that
the Dingo made himself independent of him as the
culture of the Australian degenerated. The very
factor which was probably responsible for the loss of
culture in Australian man may have contributed

towards the ultimate wildness of the Australian dog: the slowness of many marsupials and the ease with which they can be caught.

As I wished to form my own judgment upon the essence of the Dingo's being and its behaviour towards the domestic dog, I made up my mind to let one of my own bitches rear one. The opportunity presented itself when my bitch Senta, the mother of Stasi, and the Dingo bitch in Schönbrunn Zoo became pregnant at the same time.

*   *   *   *

As I was stowing the Dingo pup into my dispatch case, Antonius suddenly looked at the clock. 'Heavens above! It's time I was going! I have to go to old Werner's funeral. Aren't you going?' Of course I was going. It suddenly dawned upon me that that was the important engagement that I had had in the back of my mind all the time. Prof. Fritz Werner was one of my most respected teachers, a man whose knowledge of animals can seldom be equalled to-day. His faculty was Herpetology, that is to say he specialized in amphibians and reptiles; but besides this, he was a zoologist of great distinction, belonging to that type of scientist, now nearly extinct, which recognizes at a glance anything that creeps or flies. His knowledge was prodigious and embraced literally all classes of the animal kingdom. To accompany him on an excursion was as instructive as it was enjoyable, since he could identify without hesitation almost every form of animal life. People who were present on one of his many expeditions to North Africa and the near East, have assured me that he was as familiar with the fauna of those countries as he was with our own. Apart from this, Prof. Werner was a most successful keeper of animals and I had learned an immense amount from him on the subject of keeping terraria.

I now found myself in a situation of extreme conflict. I wanted to pay my last tribute to my honoured teacher but, at the same time, I was anxious to bring the Dingo as quickly as possible to its foster-mother in Altenberg. I felt sure that the pup would sleep contentedly in the warm nest that I had made for it in my dispatch-case, and so we set off from Schönbrunn, making our way direct to the cemetery. I had relied on being able to keep myself well in the background during the funeral ceremony; but Prof. Werner was a bachelor and had few relatives so Antonius and myself, as special students of the deceased, were obliged to walk amongst the first mourners behind the coffin. Then, as we stood in genuine sorrow by the open grave of the old zoologist, a high, penetrating cry suddenly arose from the depths of the dispatch case, the voice of a lonely puppy calling for its mother. I opened the case and inserted my hand to pacify the little Dingo but the cries only increased in intensity. There was nothing for it but to flee. I edged my way through the dense crowd of mourners, Antonius, true friend that he was, following me. First he suppressed his laughter, then he said, 'All those present were offended with you for this—except old Werner', and as he spoke there were tears in his eyes. And indeed, who knows if, amongst all those mourners at the graveside, we two, with our Dingo in the dispatch-case, were not the nearest soul-mates of the old Professor.

*   *   *   *

I arrived in Altenberg with my dispatch-case and went straight to the terrace which, for the time being, was serving as a breeding kennel to accommodate

Senta and her litter, and presented the bitch with the Australian cuckoo's egg. In the meanwhile, the Dingo had become very hungry and whined and whimpered incessantly. Senta had already heard him from a distance and now she came forward with pricked ears and a worried expression. Dogs do not see well and Senta's mental powers were not acute enough for her to realize that none of her own babies was missing. The plaintive cries from inside the case released all her maternal instincts and for all she knew the invisible pup was just another of her own puppies.

I took the Dingo out of the bag and put him on the ground in the middle of the terrace in the hope that Senta would herself carry him into her bed. If one wants a mammal mother to adopt a strange baby, it is always advisable to present her with it outside her nest and in as helpless a form as possible. The tiny helpless thing lying there forlorn stimulates the female's brood-tending instinct much more strongly than one already in the nest, and a foster-mother is quite likely to carry a foundling tenderly into her bed if the little orphan is set down outside it but will look upon it as an intruder and proceed to devour it if she finds it among her own young. To a certain extent, this kind of behaviour is also understandable from a human point of view.

The carrying of a strange baby into the nest is, however, no guarantee that it will ultimately be adopted. In the lower mammals, such as rats and mice, it often happens that a strange baby, lying outside the nest, elicits the carrying reaction, but that later when it is already in the nest, it is recognized as an intruder and remorselessly devoured. Still more reflex-like and, from a human point of view, more inconsequent, appears the maternal life-saving

reaction in many birds. Suppose, for example, that a shelduck who is leading her own brood is shown a mallard duckling crying desperately for help in the hands of the experimenter: the mother shelduck will immediately attack him with amazing courage, literally tearing the mallard duckling out of his hands. The moment after, however, when the rescued baby attempts to mingle with her own ducklings, she will set on it and, if not prevented, will kill it within a few minutes. The explanation of this contradictory behaviour is quite simple: the cries for help of the young mallard are nearly identical with those of the sheldrake ducklings and they stimulate by reflex the life-saving reaction in the female shelduck. Now the downy covering of the young mallard is noticeably different from that of the shelduck and so the former, recognized as a stranger amongst her ducklings, stimulates in her brood-defence reactions which are also reflex in nature. So the mallard suddenly becomes an enemy to be expelled instead of a child requiring succour. Even in a mammal of the high mental development of the dog, a similar conflict of opposing drives elicited by reflex is quite possible.

As the little Dingo lay yelping in the grass, Senta hurried up to him with the evident intention of carrying him to her nest. She did not even stop to smell him first in order to make sure that he was really her own puppy. She bent at once over the whimpering creature, her jaws widely opened ready to seize him in that strong grip with which mother dogs transport a puppy; they take it so far back into their mouth that it comes to rest behind the canine teeth where it cannot be injured by them. As Senta was about to do this, she was met by the wild, strange smell that the Dingo had brought with him from the

Zoo. Horrified, she sprang back, and, in the act, forced the air through her open mouth in such a way as to produce a sort of spitting hiss, similar to that of a cat but such as I have never heard in a dog either before or since. After backing some yards, she approached the whelp again, sniffing cautiously. It was at least a minute before she touched him with

her nose. Then she suddenly began to lick his coat wildly, with a lengthy, sucking action of her tongue which was all too familiar to me. It was the movement normally employed to remove the foetal membranes from the new-born young.

In order to explain her behaviour, I must be allowed to digress. When mammal mothers eat their young immediately after birth—a disaster which occurs in domestic animals such as pigs and rabbits, and occasionally in some farm-raised fur bearing animals, it can usually be attributed to a defect in the reactions which lead to the removal of the foetal membranes and the placenta, and the severing of the umbilical cord. When the baby is born the mother begins, with a sucking, licking movement, to lift up a fold in the membrane which encloses it large enough to be able to get a grip on it with her incisor teeth and open it with a careful nip. (The wrinkled-up nose and bared incisors in this action bear a close outward resemblance to the 'de-lousing' movements with which dogs seek to rid themselves of parasites by chewing their own skin in the hope of thereby destroying one of these pests.) Once the foetal coverings have been opened in this manner, they are drawn further and further into the mouth of the mother by the same licking and sucking movement till they are gradually swallowed; then follow the placenta and the adjoining part of the navel-cord. At this stage, the biting and sucking become slower and more careful till finally the free end of the navel-cord is twisted off like the end of a sausage and sucked dry. Here, of course, the operation must cease. Unfortunately in domestic animals, it often happens that the process does not stop here but continues; then, not only is the navel-cord devoured but the abdomen of the young is also opened at the umbilicus.

I once possessed a doe-rabbit which used to go on until she had eaten the liver of her young. Farmers and rabbit-breeders know that many sows and rabbits which habitually eat their young can be prevented from doing so if the new-born babies are removed from the mother immediately and only returned to her cleaned and dried some hours later when her impulse to devour the foetal wrappings has passed. Then it will be seen that such animals, apart from this kink in their behaviour, possess absolutely normal maternal instincts. Other mammal mothers, of many different species, which are quite normal in the expression of their drives and impulses, get rid of dead or diseased young by eating them. And the motions they use are exactly the same as those employed in the devouring of the foetal coverings, and begin, correspondingly, in the region of the navel.

I once witnessed a most impressive example of this behaviour: the Schönbrunn Zoo possessed a very yellow-flecked male jaguar and a fine black female jaguar which produced, nearly every year, a healthy litter, coal-black like the mother. This particular year, the great cat had given birth to a

single cub, which was sickly from the day of its birth.
Nevertheless, it had reached the age of about two
months at the time when I was walking through the
Zoo with Prof. Antonius. As we neared the cages of
the great beasts of prey, Antonius told me that the
young jaguar had not been thriving lately and that
he feared for its survival. We found the jaguar
mother in the act of 'washing', cat-like, her baby,
that is, of licking it all over. A lady artist, a great
animal lover and a regular visitor to the Zoo, happened to be standing by the cage and expressed her
approval of the mother's solicitude for her sick baby.
Antonius, however, shook his head sadly as he turned
to me. 'An examination question for the specialist in
animal behaviour: what is going on in the mind of
the mother jaguar?' I knew at once what he meant.
The licking showed a strange, nervous haste and a
slight tendency to sucking; I had twice noticed how
the mother shoved her nose under the belly of the
baby, aiming her tongue in the direction of the navel.
I therefore answered, 'Beginning of conflict between brood-tending reaction and impulse to devour
dead young'. The tender-hearted artist did not want
to believe it, but my friend nodded and unfortunately
I proved to be right. Next morning, the little jaguar
had disappeared without a trace. His mother had
eaten him.

All these things occurred to me as I watched the
way Senta was licking the little Dingo and I was not
mistaken in my conclusions. After a few minutes, she
shoved her nose under the puppy's belly, rolling him
over on his back. Then she began to lick carefully at
his navel and soon she was nipping the skin of his
belly with her front teeth. The Dingo cried out and
began to whimper more loudly. Again Senta jumped
back horrified as though she suddenly realized,

'I am hurting the wee thing.' It was clear that the brood-tending reaction, the 'pity' elicited by the cry of pain, had once more gained ascendancy. She made a decided movement towards the puppy's head as though she wished to carry him to her bed; but as she opened her mouth to seize him, she encountered once more the strange, unknown scent, and the hasty licking began anew, increasing in fervour until she started once more tweaking the skin of the pup's abdomen; then came the cry of pain and again the bitch recoiled in horror. Now she approached him again and this time her movements became more hurried, her licking more frantic and the exchange of opposing drives more rapid as she was swayed between carrying the orphan or devouring the unwanted, 'wrong-smelling' changeling. It was obvious what inward torment Senta was suffering, and quite suddenly she broke down altogether under the strain of the conflict: she sat back on her haunches in front of the Dingo, raised her nose to the sky, and gave vent to her distress in a long, wolf-like howl. At this juncture, I took not only the Dingo but also Senta's own young and put them all together in a narrow box which I placed near the kitchen stove. There I left them for twelve hours, to crawl over each other and intermingle their scent. When I returned them to the bitch next morning, she received them somewhat dubiously and became very excited. However, she soon transported them methodically to her kennel, and the little Dingo was taken neither first nor last but in the midst of her own puppies. But later on she recognized him as a stranger and, though she did not turn him out and even suckled him with her own, one day she bit him so severely in the ear that it never properly recovered its shape and ever after drooped to one side.

13. WHAT A PITY HE CAN'T SPEAK—
HE UNDERSTANDS EVERY WORD

And then, his nature, how impressionable,
How quickly moved to Collie mirth or woe,
Elated or dejected at a word!

WILLIAM WATSON

IT is a fallacy to suppose that domestic animals are less intelligent than the wild forms from which they originated. Certainly their senses have in many cases become blunter and some of their instincts dulled, but this applies to man also, and it is not despite these losses but because of them that man is superior to animals. The dulling of the instincts and of the fixed paths along which much of animal behaviour runs was the prerequisite for the rise of a certain, specifically human, freedom of action. In the domestic animal also, the decline of various innate behaviour reactions implies a new degree of freedom and not a lessening of the capacity to act rationally. In 1898, C. O. Whitman, the first man to understand and to make a study of these things, said, 'These defects in the instinct are not in themselves intelligence but they are the open door through which the great teacher, Experience, can enter and bring about all the wonders of the intellect.'

Expressive movements and the social reactions which they elicit belong to the instinctive, inherited behaviour patterns of a species. Everything that socially living animals such as jackdaws, greylag geese, canine beasts of prey, 'have to say' to each other belongs exclusively to the plane of those interlocking norms of action and reaction which are innate in the animals of a species. R. Schenkel has recently examined the expressive movements of the wolf and analysed their meaning. If we compare the 'vocabulary' of signals which the wolf has at its disposal for social intercourse with those of our domestic dogs, we find in the latter the same signs of disintegration and decay as can be seen in so many other innate specific behaviour patterns. It is open to question whether these movements are not already less clearly defined in the jackal than in the wolf, but quite conceivable, since the social structure of the latter is doubtlessly much more highly developed. In lupus blooded dogs like Chows, all the forms of expression of the wolf are to be found, excepting those signals which are expressed by the movements and carriage of the tail. The Chow, with its curly tail, is mechanically incapable of making these movements, nevertheless it transmits to its descendant an innate tendency to make specific wolfish tail signals. All those dogs of my cross-bred stud which have inherited from the Alsatian side a normal 'wild-formed' stern make all the typical tail movements of the wolf which are never seen in pure Alsatians and other more or less jackal-blooded dogs.

In their innate expressive movements, in the miming of their facial muscles, and in the carriage of body and tail, some of my dogs approach more closely to the wolf than do any other European dogs. But even my dogs are less well equipped in this respect than the wolf, their facial expression being less marked than that of the wild form, although it is incomparably more so than that of most other dogs. To the experienced jackal dog-lover this statement will seem almost paradoxical for he will no doubt be thinking of general powers of expression, while it is the innate movements that I am discussing. The principle mentioned above, that the decline of the fixed innate opens new possibilities for 'freely invented' behaviour patterns is nowhere so clearly shown as in the faculty of expression. Almost like the wolf, the Chow is restricted to those miming movements by which wild animals display to each other feelings such as anger, submissiveness or joy, and these movements are not very conspicuous, since they are attuned to the extremely fine reacting mechanism of the wild members of the species. Man has largely lost these reactions, for he possesses in the language of words a coarser but more easily intelligible form of communication. Endowed with the power of speech he is not obliged to 'read in the eyes' of his fellows every slight change of mood. To most people, wild animals also appear limited in expression, although just the contrary is the case. The Chow is inscrutable to people accustomed to jackal dogs, just as the face of many eastern Asiatics is impenetrable to most Europeans. But a trained eye can detect in the unrevealing countenance of a wolf or Chow just as much as in the demonstrative facial expressions of a jackal dog. The latter are, however, on a higher mental plane: they are largely independent of the innate and have mostly been learnt or freely invented by the individual animal. No fixed instinct impels a dog to express his affection by laying his head on his master's knee, and it is for this reason that such an action is more nearly related to our human language

H

than anything that wild animals 'say' to each other.

Still more closely related to the power of speech is the use of learned action as an expression of feeling, as for example giving the paw. Many dogs which have learned this do it to their master in a definite social situation as when they wish to conciliate him or to ask his forgiveness. Everybody has seen the dog which, having misbehaved, crawls to his master and sitting down before him with ears laid back and extreme 'humiliation face', crampedly tries to offer his paw. I once knew a poodle which even did this to another dog; but this was a rare exception, for when 'speaking' to their own kind, even dogs with a large repertory of individually acquired expressions only use the innate miming of the wild form. Of dogs in general one may say that the greater their faculty for independent, acquired or freely 'invented' expression the less they retain of the specific miming peculiar to the wild form of the species. Thus the most highly domesticated dogs are generally the most free and adaptable in their behaviour, though individual intelligence is also an important factor. A particularly intelligent dog of a type approaching the wild form may, under certain conditions, invent better and more complex ways of making itself understood than a dog with fewer wild instincts and less sagacity. The absence of instinct is merely the open door for intelligence and never intelligence itself.

What has been said about the ability of the dog to express its feelings towards man applies in a still higher degree to its capacity for understanding human gestures and language. We may take it for granted that those hunters who were the first people to establish a social contact with almost completely wild dogs had a finer perception of animal expressive movements than a present day town dweller. Up to a point this was part of their professional training, for a stone-age hunter who could not distinguish a peaceful from an angry mood in a cave-bear would indeed have been a bungler. This faculty in man was not instinct but a feat of learning, and the same is required of a dog which is expected to understand human expressions and language. The innate ability of an animal to understand expressive movements and sounds only extends to those of nearly related species, and inexperienced dogs even fail to understand the miming of felines. Considering this fact, the degree to which dogs understand human expressions of feeling is little short of a miracle.

Much as I love Lupus dogs in general and Chows in particular, I have no doubt that all the more highly domesticated jackal dogs are much better at understanding their masters in most feelings. My Alsatian bitch, Tito, far surpassed all her lupus-blooded descendants in this respect, for she knew at once whom I liked and whom I disliked. Amongst my cross-bred dogs, I have always preferred those that inherited this perceptiveness. Stasi, for instance, reacted to any symptoms of illness, and expressed her anxiety not only when I had a headache or a chill but also when I was feeling downhearted. She would demonstrate her sympathy by a less cheerful gait than usual, and with subdued demeanour would keep strictly to heel, gazing up at me continually and pressing her shoulder against my knee whenever I stood still. It was interesting that she behaved in the same way if ever I had drunk a little more than was good for me, and so perturbed did she become over my 'illness' that her concern would have been enough to prevent my taking to drink had I ever

been inclined that way. Though my dogs, thanks to their Alsatian inheritance, possess in wide measure the power to understand and to make themselves understood, there is no doubt that these faculties are incomparably better developed in some highly domesticated jackal dogs. As far as I can generalize from my own canine acquaintances, I should give the Poodle, rightly famed for his sagacity, the first place, next I should put the Alsatian, certain Pinschers and large Schnauzers; but for my own personal taste all these dogs have lost too much of the primitive nature of the beast of prey. Owing to their extraordinary 'humanness' they lack that charm of the natural which characterizes my wild 'wolves'.

It is a fallacy that dogs only understand the tone of a word and are deaf to the articulation. The well-known animal psychologist, Sarris, proved this indisputably with three Alsatians, called Harris, Aris and Paris. On command from their master, 'Harris (Aris, Paris), Go to your basket', the dog addressed and that one only would get up unfailingly and walk sadly but obediently to his bed. The order was carried out just as faithfully when it was issued from the next room whence an accompanying involuntary signal was out of the question. It sometimes seems to me that the word recognition of a clever dog which is firmly attached to its master extends even to whole sentences. The words, 'I must go now' would bring Tito and Stasi to their feet at once even when I exercised great self-control and spoke without special accentuation; on the other hand, none of these words, spoken in a different connection, elicited any response from them.

It was a big Schnauzer bitch, Affi, which, of all the dogs I have known, held the record for understanding human words. She belonged to the coillustrator of this book of whose truthfulness I am quite confident. This sporting creature reacted differently to the words, 'Katzi, Spatzi, Nazi, and Eichkatzi' (diminutives of, kitten, sparrow; Nazi had no political meaning in those days and was the name of the owner's pet hedgehog, squirrel). The dog's owner had thus, without knowing of Sarris' experiments, accomplished a largely analogous research result: on the word 'Katzi', Affi's hackles bristled and she sniffed the floor in a state of excitement which displayed her unmistakable anticipation of a prey likely to defend itself. Sparrows she only chased in her youth; in later life, when she had realized the hopelessness of the task, she would look out for them without moving and gaze boredly after them. She hated Nazi the hedgehog although she did not recognize him as an individual, but, upon mention of his name she would rush to the rubbish heap where another hedgehog lived and begin to rummage amongst the leaves and to give tongue in that furious way in which dogs vent their helpless rage on that painfully prickly creature. This unequivocal high-pitched yap would be produced on command even if no hedgehog was present. At the word, 'Eichkatzi', Affi looked upwards expectantly and if she saw no squirrel she dashed from tree to tree looking for one; like many dogs with a poor scent she had excellent sight and saw better and further than most of her kind. She also understood signals made by hand, a thing few dogs are able to do; and she knew the names of at least nine people, and would run across the room to them if their names were spoken. She never made a mistake.

Should these experiments seem incredible to the animal psychologist who works in the laboratory, he must consider the fact that the experimental animal in a confined space has fewer experiences which he can differentiate qualitatively than does the dog which is always free to accompany his master. It is much more difficult for a dog to associate with a certain word a corresponding feat of training which does not excite his interest, than it is for him to link up a word with such a stimulating prey as any of the above four. With the dog, one is seldom given the chance of achieving high feats of word recognition in the laboratory, since the necessary interest is lacking: the 'valencies' in the sense of animal psychology are not present in sufficient quantity. Every dog-owner is familiar with a certain behaviour in dogs which can never be produced under laboratory conditions. The owner says, without special intonation and avoiding mention of the dog's name, 'I don't know whether I'll take him or not.' At once the dog is on the spot, wagging his tail and dancing with excitement, for he already senses a walk. Had his master said, 'I suppose I must take him out now,' the dog would have got up resignedly without special interest. Should his master say, 'I don't think I'll take him, after all,' the expectantly pricked ears will drop sadly, though the dog's eyes will remain hopefully fixed on his master. On the final pronouncement, 'I'll leave him at home', the dog turns dejectedly away and lies down again. Imagine what complicated experimental methods and how tiresome a training would be necessary in order to achieve an analogous result under artificial conditions in the laboratory.

Unfortunately, I have never had a real friendship with one of the large anthropoid apes. But Mrs Hayes has done so and has shown that a very close social contact, enduring for many years, is possible between man and ape. Such a close contact, especially between a critical and experienced scientist and an animal bound to him by the close ties of mutual affection, is the best test for the intellectual capacities of these creatures. It is certainly too early to compare the dog with anthropoid apes but personally I believe the dog would prove better at understanding human talk however much the ape may surpass him in other feats of intelligence. In a certain respect, the dog is more 'human' than the cleverest monkeys: like man, he is a domesticated being, and like him, he owes to his domestication two constitutional properties: first his liberation from the fixed tracks of instinctive behaviour which opens to him, as to man, new ways of acting; and secondly, that persistent youthfulness, which in the dog is the root of his permanent longing for affection, but which in man preserves even into ripe old age that universal open mindedness which caused Wordsworth to say,

WHAT A PITY
HE CAN'T
SPEAK—HE
UNDERSTANDS
EVERY WORD

137

> *So was it when my life began,*
> *So is it now I am a man,*
> *So be it when I shall grow old,*
> *Or let me die.*

14. AFFECTION'S CLAIM

Knowing me in my soul the very same—
One who would die to spare you touch of ill!—
Will you not grant to old affection's claim
The hand of friendship down Life's
sunless hill?

THOMAS HARDY

I ONCE possessed a fascinating little book of crazy tales called 'Snowshoe Al's Bedtime Stories'. It concealed behind a mask of ridiculous nonsense that penetrating and somewhat cruel satire which is one of the characteristic features of American humour, and which is not always easily intelligible to many Europeans. In one of these stories Snowshoe Al relates with romantic sentimentality the heroic deeds of his best friend. Incidents of incredible courage, exaggerated manliness and complete altruism are piled up in a comical parody of Western American romanticism culminating in the touching scenes where the hero saves his friend's life from wolves, grizzly bears, hunger, cold and all the manifold dangers which beset him. The story ends with the laconic statement, 'In so doing, his feet became so badly frozen that I unfortunately had to shoot him.'

If I ask a man who has just been boasting of the prowess and other wonderful properties of one of his dogs, I always ask him whether he has still got the animal. The answer, then, is all too often strongly reminiscent of Snowshoe Al's story, "No, I had to get rid of him—I moved to another town—or into a smaller house—I got another job and it was awkward for me to keep a dog,' or some other similar excuse. It is to me amazing that many people who are otherwise morally sound feel no disgrace in admitting such an action. They do not realize that there is no difference between their behaviour and that of the satirized egoist in the story. The animal is deprived of rights, not only by the letter of the law, but also by many people's insensitivity.

The fidelity of a dog is a precious gift demanding no less binding moral responsibilities than the friendship of a human being. The bond with a true dog is as lasting as the ties of this earth can ever be, a fact which should be noted by anyone who decides to acquire a canine friend. It may of course happen that the love of a dog is thrust upon one involuntarily, a circumstance which occurred to me when I met the Hanoverian Schweisshund, 'Hirschmann', on a ski-ing tour. He was at the time about a year old and a typical masterless dog; for his owner, the head forester only loved his old Deutscher Rauhaar (German Pointer) and had no time for the clumsy stripling which showed few signs of ever becoming a gun-dog. Hirschmann was soft and sensitive and a little shy of his master, a fact which did not speak highly for the training ability of the forester. On the other hand I did not think any the better of the dog for coming out with us as early as the second day of our stay. I took him for a sycophant, quite wrongly as it turned out, for he was following not us but me alone. When one morning I found him sleeping outside my bedroom door, I began to reconsider my first opinion and to suspect that a great canine love was

germinating. I realized it too late: the oath of allegiance had been sworn nor would the dog recant on
the day of my departure. I tried to catch him in
order to shut him up and prevent him from following
us, but he refused to come near me. Quivering with
consternation and with his tail between his legs, he
stood at a safe distance saying with his eyes, 'I'll do
anything at all for you—except leave you!' I capit-
ulated. 'Forester, what's the price of your dog?' The
forester, from whose point of view the dog's conduct
was sheer desertion, replied without a moment's consideration, 'Ten shillings.' It sounded like an ex-
pletive and was meant as such. Before he could think
of a better one, the ten shillings were in his hand and
two pairs of skis and two pairs of dog's paws were
under way. I knew that Hirschmann would follow us
but surmised erroneously that, plagued by his
conscience, he would slink after us at a distance,
thinking that he was not allowed to come with us.
What really did happen was entirely unexpected.
The full weight of the huge dog hit me broadsides
on like a cannon ball and I was precipitated hip fore-
most on to the icy road. A skier's equilibrium is not
proof against the impact of an enormous dog, hurled
in a delirium of excitement against him. I had quite
underestimated his grasp of the situation. As for
Hirschmann, he danced for joy over my extended
corpse.

I have always taken very seriously the responsibility imposed by a dog's fidelity, and I am proud
that I once risked my life, though inadvertently, to
save a dog which had fallen into the Danube at a
temperature of $-28°$ C. My Alsatian, Bingo, was
running along the frozen edge of the river when he
slipped and fell into the water. His claws were unable

to grip the sides of the ice so he could not get out.
Dogs become exhausted very quickly when attempting to get up too steep a bank. They get into an awkward, more and more upright swimming position
until they are soon in imminent danger of drowning.
I therefore ran a few yards ahead of the dog which
was being swept downstream; then I lay down and,
in order to distribute my weight, crept on my belly to
the edge of the ice. As Bingo came within my reach,
I seized him by the scruff of the neck and pulled him
with a jerk towards me on to the ice, but our joint
weight was too much for it—it broke, and I slid
silently, head first into the freezing cold water. The
dog, which, unlike myself, had its head shorewards,
managed to reach firmer ice. Now the situation was
reversed; Bingo ran apprehensively along the ice and
I floated downstream in the current. Finally, because
the human hand is better adapted than the paw of
the dog for gripping a smooth surface, I managed to
escape disaster by my own efforts. I felt ground beneath my feet and threw my upper half upon the ice.

We judge the moral worth of two human friends
according to which of them is ready to make the
greater sacrifice without thought of recompense.
Nietzsche who, unlike most people, wore brutality
only as a mask to hide true warmness of heart, said
the beautiful words, 'Let it be your aim always to
love more than the other, never to be the second.'
With human beings, I am sometimes able to fulfil
this commandment, but in my relations with a faithful dog, I am always the second. What a strange and
unique social relationship! Have you ever thought
how extraordinary it all is? Man, endowed with
reason and a highly developed sense of moral responsibility, whose finest and noblest belief is the

religion of brotherly love, in this very respect falls short of the carnivores. In saying this I am not indulging in sentimental anthropomorphization. Even the noblest human love arises, not from reason and the specifically human, rational moral sense, but from the much deeper age-old layers of instinctive feeling. The highest and most selfless moral behaviour loses all value in our estimation when it arises not from such sources but from the reason. Elizabeth Browning said,

> *If thou must love me, let it be for nought*
> *Except for love's sake only.*

Even to-day man's heart is still the same as that of the higher social animals, no matter how far the achievements of his reason and his rational moral sense transcend theirs. The plain fact that my dog loves me more than I love him is undeniable and always fills me with a certain feeling of shame. The dog is ever ready to lay down his life for me. If a lion or a tiger threatened me, Ali, Bully, Tito, Stasi, and all the others would, without a moment's hesitation, have plunged into the hopeless fight to protect my life if only for a few seconds. And I?

15. DOG DAYS

The brilliant smell of water,
The brave smell of a stone.

G. K. CHESTERTON: *Quoodle's Song*

I DO not know how the dog days got their name.
I believe from Sirius the dog star, but the
etymological origin of the North German synonym,
the 'Sauregurkenzeit' (sour cucumber time), seems
much more appropriate. But for me personally, the
dog days could not be better named, because I
make a habit of spending them in the exclusive
company of my dog. When I am fed to the teeth
with brain work, when clever talk and politeness
nearly drive me distracted, when the very sight
of a typewriter fills me with revulsion, all of which
sentiments generally overtake me at the end of a
normal summer term, then I decide to 'go to the
dogs'. I retire from human society and seek that of
animals—and for this reason: I know almost no
human being who is lazy enough to keep me company in such a mood, for I possess the priceless gift
of being able, when in a state of great contentment,
to shut off my higher thinking powers completely,
and this is the essential condition for perfect peace of
mind. When, on a hot summer day, I swim across
the Danube and lie in a dreamy backwater of the

great river, like a crocodile in the mud, amongst
scenery that shows not the slightest sign of the existence of human civilization, then I sometimes achieve
that miraculous state which is the highest goal of
oriental sages. Without going to sleep, my higher
centres dissolve into a strange at-oneness with surrounding nature; my thoughts stand still, time ceases
to mean anything and, when the sun begins to sink
and the cool of the evening warns me that I have
still another three and a half miles to swim home, I
do not know whether seconds or years have passed
since I crawled out on to the muddy bank.

This animal nirvana is an unequalled panacea for
mental strain, true balm for the mind of hurried,
worried, modern man, which has been rubbed sore
in so many places. I do not always succeed in
achieving this healing return to the thoughtless
happiness of pre-human paradise but I am most
likely to do so in the company of an animal which is
still a rightful participant of it. Thus there are very
definite and deep-rooted reasons why I need a dog
which accompanies me faithfully but which has retained a wild exterior and thus does not spoil the
landscape by its civilized appearance.

Yesterday morning at dawn, it was already
so hot that work—mental work—seemed hopeless—
a heaven sent Danube day! I left my room armed
with fishing net and glass jar, in order to catch and
carry the live food which I always bring home for
my fishes from every Danube excursion. As always,
this is an unmistakable sign for Susi that a dog day,
a happy dog day is pending. She is quite convinced
that I undertake these expeditions for her exclusive
benefit and perhaps she is not altogether wrong. She
knows that I not only allow her to go with me but
that I set the greatest store by her company; never-

theless, to be quite sure of not being left behind, she presses close to my legs all the way to the yard gate.

theless, to be quite sure of not being left behind, she
presses close to my legs all the way to the yard gate.
Then, with proudly raised bushy tail, she trots down
the village street before me, her dancing, elastic gait
showing all the village dogs that she is afraid of none
of them, even when Wolf II is not with her. With
the horribly ugly mongrel belonging to the village
grocer—I hope he will never read this book—she
usually has a short flirtation. To the deep disgust of
Wolf II, she loves this checkered creature more than
any other dog, but to-day she has no time for him,
and when he attempts to play with her she wrinkles
her nose and bares her gleaming teeth at him before
trotting on to growl, according to her custom, at her
various enemies behind their different garden fences.

The village street is still in the shade and its hard
ground is cold beneath my bare feet, but beyond the
railway bridge, the deep dust of the path to the river
presses itself, caressingly warm, between my toes, and
above the footprints of the dog trotting in front of
me, it rises in little clouds in the still air. Crickets and
cicada chirp merrily and, on the nearby river bank,
a golden oriole and a black-cap are singing. Thank
goodness that they are still singing—that summer is
still young enough. Our way leads over a freshly
mown meadow and Susi leaves the path, for this is a
special 'mousing' meadow. Her trot becomes a
curious, stiff-legged slink, she carries her head very
high, her whole expression betraying her excitement,
and her tail sinks low, stretched out behind, close
above the ground. Altogether she resembles a rather
too fat blue Arctic fox. Suddenly, as though released
by a spring, she shoots in a semicircle about a yard
high and two yards forwards. Landing on her fore-
paws close together and stiffly outstretched, she bites
several times, quick as lightning, into the short grass.

With loud snorts she bores her pointed nose into the ground, then, raising her head, she looks question-ingly in my direction, her tail wagging all the time: the mouse has gone. She certainly feels ashamed when her tremendous mouse jump misses its mark, and she is equally proud if she catches her prey. Now she slinks further on and four further leaps fall short of their goal—voles are amazingly quick and agile. But now the little Chow bitch flies through the air like a rubber ball and as her paws touch the ground there follows a high-pitched, painfully sharp squeak. She bites again, then, with a hurried shaking move-ment, drops what she was biting, and a small, grey body flies in a semicircle through the air with Susi, in a larger semicircle, after it. Snapping several times, with retracted lips, she seizes, with her incisors only, something squeaking and struggling in the grass. Then she turns to me and shows me the big, fat, distorted fieldmouse that she is holding in her jaws. I praise her roundly and declare that she is a most terrifying, awe-inspiring animal for whom one must have the greatest respect. I am sorry for the vole but I did not know it personally, and Susi is my bosom friend whose triumphs I feel bound to share. Nevertheless, my conscience is easier when she eats it, thereby vindicating herself by the only action that can ever justify killing. First she gingerly chews it with her incisors only to a formless but still intact mass, then she takes it far back into her mouth and begins to gobble it up and swallow it. And now for the time being she has had enough of mousing and suggests to me that we should proceed.

Our path leads to the river, where I undress and hide my clothes and fishing tackle. From here the track goes upstream, following the old tow-path where in former times horses used to pull the barges up the river. But now the path is so overgrown that only

a narrow strip remains which leads through a thick
forest of golden rod, mixed unpleasantly with solitary
nettles and blackberry bushes, so that one needs both
arms to keep the stinging pricking vegetation from
one's body. The damp heat in this plant wilderness is
truly unbearable and Susi walks panting at my heels,
quite indifferent to any hunting prospects that the
undergrowth may hold. I can understand her apathy
because I am dripping with sweat, and I pity her in
her thick fur coat. At last we reach the place where
I wish to cross the river. At the present low level of
the river a wide shingle bank stretches far out into
the current and, as I pick my way somewhat painfully over the stones, Susi runs ahead joyfully and
plunges breast high into the water where she lies
down till only her head remains visible: a queer little
angular outline against the vast expanse of the river.

As I wade out into the current, the dog presses
close behind me and whines softly. She has never yet
crossed the Danube and its width fills her with mis-
giving. I speak reassuringly to her and wade in
further, but she is obliged to start swimming when
the water reaches barely to my knees and she is
carried rapidly downstream. In order to keep up
with her, I begin to swim too, although it is far too
shallow for me, but the fact that I am now travelling
as swiftly as she is reassures her and she swims
steadily by my side. A dog that will swim alongside
its master shows particular intelligence: many dogs
can never realize the fact that in the water a man is
not upright as it is used to seeing him, with the
unpleasant result that in an attempt to keep close
behind the head on the surface of the water, it
scratches its master's back horribly with its wildly
paddling paws.

But Susi has immediately grasped the fact that a man swims horizontally and she carefully avoids coming too near to me from behind. She is nervous in the broad, sweeping river and keeps as close beside me as possible. Now her anxiety reaches such a pitch that she rears up out of the water and looks back at the bank we have left behind us. I am afraid that she may turn back altogether but she settles down again, swimming quietly at my side. Soon another difficulty arises: in her excitement and in the effort to cross the great, wide current as quickly as possible, she strikes out at a speed which I cannot indefinitely maintain. Panting, I strain to keep up with her, but she outstrips me again and again, only to turn round and swim back to me every time she finds herself a few yards ahead. There is always the danger that, on sighting our home shore, she will leave me and return to it, since for an animal in a state of apprehension the direction of home exerts a much stronger pull than any other. In any case, dogs find it hard to alter course while swimming, so that I am relieved when I have persuaded her to turn again in the right direction and, swimming with all my might to keep close behind her, to send her on again each time she tries to come back. The fact that she understands my encouragement and is influenced by it is fresh proof to me that her intelligence is well above the average.

We land on a sandbank which is steeper than the one we have just left. Susi is some yards in front of me, and as she climbs out of the water and makes her first few steps on dry land I see that she sways

noticeably to and fro. This slight disturbance of balance, which passes in a few seconds and which I myself often experience after a longer swim, is known to many swimmers, who have confirmed my observation. But I can find no satisfactory physiological explanation for it. Although I have repeatedly noticed it in dogs, I have never seen it in such a marked degree as Susi showed on this occasion. The condition has nothing to do with exhaustion, which fact Susi at once makes clear to me by expressing in no uncertain measure her joy at having conquered the stream. She bursts forth in an ecstasy of joy, races in small circles round my legs and finally fetches a stick for me to throw for her, a game into which I willingly enter. When she grows tired of it, she rushes off at top speed after a wagtail which is sitting on the shore some fifty yards away: not that she naïvely expects to catch the bird, for she knows quite well that wagtails like to fly along the river bank and that, when they have gained a few dozen yards, they sit down again, thus making excellent pacemakers for a short hunt.

I am glad that my little friend is in such a happy mood, for it means much to me that she should often come on these swimming expeditions across the Danube. For this reason, I wish to reward her amply for her first crossing of the river, and there is no better way of doing this than by taking her for a long walk through the delightful virgin wilderness flanking the shores of the river. One can learn a lot when

wandering through this wilderness with an animal friend, particularly if one lets oneself be guided by its tastes and interests.

First we walk upstream along the river's edge, then we follow the course of a little backwater which, at its lower end, is clear and deep; further on, it breaks up into a chain of little pools, which become shallower and shallower as we proceed. A strangely tropical effect is produced by these backwaters. The banks descend in wild luxuriance, steeply, almost vertically, to the water, and are begirt by a regular botanical garden of high willows, poplars and oaks between which hang dense strands of lush wood vine, like lianas; kingfishers and golden orioles, also typical denizens of this landscape, both belong to groups of birds, the majority of whose members are tropical dwellers. In the water grows thick swamp vegetation. Tropical too is the damp heat which hangs over this wonderful jungle landscape, which can only be borne with comfort and dignity by a naked man who spends more time in the water than out of it; and finally let us not deny that malaria mosquitoes and numerous gad-flies play their part in enhancing the tropical impression.

In the broad band of mud that frames the backwater the tracks of many riverside dwellers can be seen, as though cast in plaster, and their visiting cards are printed in the hard-baked clay until the next rainfall or high water. Who says that there are no more stags left in the Danube swamps? Judging by the hoof-prints, there must still be many large ones, although they are scarcely ever heard at rutting time, so furtive have they become since the perils of the last war whose final, terrible phases took place in these very woods. Foxes and deer, musk-rats and smaller rodents, countless common

sandpipers, wood sandpipers and little ringed plovers, have decorated the mud with the inter-woven chains of their footsteps. And if these tracks are full of interest for my eyes, how much more so must they be for the nose of my little Chow bitch! She revels in scent orgies of which we poor noseless ones can have no conception, for 'Goodness only knowses the noselessness of man'. The tracks of stags and large deer do not interest her, for, thank heaven, Susi is no big game hunter, being far too obsessed with her passion for mousing.

But the scent of a musk-rat is a different thing: slinking tremulously, her nose close to the ground and her tail stretched obliquely upwards and backwards, she follows these rodents to the very entrance of their burrows which, owing to the present low water are above instead of below the water line. She applies her nose to the holes, greedily inhaling the delicious smell of game, and she even begins the hopeless task of digging up the burrow, which pleasure I do not deny her. I lie flat on my stomach, in the shallow, luke-warm water, letting the sun burn down on my back and I am in no hurry to move on. At last Susi turns towards me a face plastered with earth; wagging her tail, she walks panting towards me and, with a deep sigh, lies down beside me in the water. So we remain for nearly an hour, at the end of which time she gets up and begs me to go on. We pursue the ever drier course of the backwater upstream, and now we turn a bend and beside another pool, quite unconscious of our presence, for the wind is against us, is a huge musk-rat: the apotheosis of all Susi's dreams, a gigantic, a god-like rat, a rat of un-precedented dimensions. The dog freezes to a statue and I do likewise. Then, slowly as a chameleon, step by step, she begins to stalk the wonder beast.

She gets amazingly far, covering almost half the distance which separates us from the rat; and it is tremendously thrilling for there is always the chance that, in its first bewilderment, it may jump into the pool which has shrunk away into its stony bed and has no outlet. The creature's burrow must be at least some yards away from the spot, on the level of the normal water-line. But I have underestimated the intelligence of the rat. All of a sudden he sees the dog and streaks like lightning across the mud in the direction of the bank, Susi after him like a shot from a gun. She is clever enough not to pursue him in a straight line but to try to cut him off at a tangent, on his way to cover. Simultaneously she lets out a passionate cry such as I have rarely heard from a dog. Perhaps if she had not given tongue and had instead applied her whole energy to the chase she might have got him, for she is but half a yard behind as he disappears into safety.

Expecting Susi to dig for ages at the mouth of the earth, I lie down in the mud of the pool, but she only sniffs longingly at the entrance, then turns away disappointedly and rejoins me in the water. We both feel that the day has reached its climax: golden orioles sing, frogs croak, and great dragonflies, with a dry whirr of their glossy wings, chase the gad-flies which are tormenting us. Good luck to their hunting! So we lie nearly all afternoon and I succeed in being more animal than any animal or at any rate much lazier than my dog, in fact as lazy as any crocodile. This bores Susi and, having nothing better to do, she begins to chase the frogs which, made bold by our long inertia, have resumed their activities. She stalks the nearest one, trying out her mouse-jump technique in the attempt to kill this new prey. But her paws land with a splash in the water and the frog dives away unhurt. Shaking the water from her eyes, she looks around to see where the frog has got to. She sees it, or thinks she does, in the middle of the pool where the rounded shoots of a water mint appear, to the imperfect eye-sight of a dog, not unlike the head of a squatting frog. Susi eyes the object, holding her head first on the left side then on the right, then slowly, very slowly, she wades into the water, swims up to the plant and bites at it. Looking round with a long suffering air to see if I am laughing at her absurd mistake, she turns about and finally swims back to the bank and lies down beside me. I ask, 'Shall we go home?' and Susi springs up, answering 'Yes' with all her available means of expression. We push our way through the jungle, straight ahead to the river. We are a long way upstream from Altenberg but the current carries us at the rate of nearly twelve miles an hour. Susi shows no more fear of the great expanse of water, and she swims quietly beside me, letting the stream carry her along. We land close by my clothes and fishing tackle and hastily I catch a delicious supper for the fish in my aquaria. Then in the dusk, satisfied and happy, we return home the same way as we came. In the mousing meadow, Susi has better luck, for she catches no less than three fat voles in succession—a compensation for her failure with the musk-rat and the frog.

To-day I must go to Vienna, although the heat forecasts another 'dog day'. I must take this chapter to the publisher. No, Susi, you cannot come with me, you can see I've got long trousers on. But to-morrow, to-morrow, Susi, we'll swim the Danube again and, if we try very hard, perhaps we'll even catch that musk-rat.

16. ON FELINE PLAY

As though his whole vocation
Were endless imitation.

WORDSWORTH:
Ode on the Intimations of Immortality

THERE are certain things in Nature in which beauty and utility, artistic and technical perfection, combine in some incomprehensible way: the web of a spider, the wing of a dragon-fly, the superbly streamlined body of the porpoise, and the movements of a cat. These last could not be lovelier even had they been designed by a preternaturally gifted dancer striving for choreographic grace, nor could they be more practical even under the tuition of that best of all 'coaches'—the struggle for existence. And it is almost as though the animal were aware of the beauty of its movements, for it appears to delight in them and to perform them for the sake of their own perfection. This game, the game of movements, occupies a very special place in the life of this most elegant of all animals.

What 'play' really is is one of the most difficult questions in animal and human psychology. We know exactly what we mean when we say that a kitten, a puppy or a child is playing, but it is very difficult to give a real definition of this highly significant activity. All forms of play have the common quality that they are fundamentally different from 'earnest'; at the same time, however, they show an unmistakable resemblance, indeed an imitation of a definite, earnest situation. This even holds good for the abstract games of grown men, certain definite, intellectual capacities and abilities finding expression in their poker or chess matches. In spite of these basic similarities however, 'play' is an enormously wide conception. It embraces activities as different as the stiff, hard-and-fast ceremonial of a baroque minuet, and the carpentering efforts of a growing boy. It is 'play' when a young rabbit runs and doubles back from sheer ebullience, although no predatory beast is after him, and it is play when a little boy pretends to be an engine-driver. The reader is probably beginning to fear that I am lapsing into an abstract lecture on the common properties of these human and animal activities, which entitle us to give them the same name. But I will return to the theme of the chapter heading: feline play. Perhaps some observations of a real case will give us some helpful clues for the elucidation of the problems of play.

A kitten is playing with its classical plaything, a ball of wool. Invariably it begins by pawing at the object, first gently and enquiringly with outstretched fore-arm and inwardly flexed paw. Then, with extended claws, it draws the ball towards itself, pushes it away again or jumps a few steps backwards, crouching. It lies low, raises its head with tense expression, glaring at the plaything. Then its head drops so suddenly that you expect its chin to bump the floor. The hind feet perform peculiar, alternately treading and clawing movements as though the kitten were seeking a firm hold from which to spring. Suddenly it bounds in a great semicircle and lands

on its toy with stiff fore-paws, pressed closely together. It will even bite it, if the game has reached a pitch of some intensity. Again it pushes the ball and this time it rolls under a cupboard which stands too close to the floor for the kitten to get underneath. With an elegant 'practised' movement, it reaches with one arm into the space and fishes its plaything out again. It is at once clear to anyone who has ever watched a cat catching a mouse, that our kitten, which we have reared apart from its mother, is performing all those highly specialized movements which aid the cat in the hunting of its most important prey—the mouse. In the wild state, this constitutes its 'daily bread'.

If we now improve on our plaything by attaching a thread to it and letting it dangle from above, the kitten will exhibit entirely different prey-catching movements. Jumping high, it grabs the prey with both paws at once, bringing them together in a wide, sweeping movement from the sides. During this movement, the paws appear abnormally large, for all the digits with their extended claws are widely spread, and the dew-claws are bent at right angles to the paw. This grasping movement, which many kittens delightedly perform in play, is identical to the last detail with the movement used by cats to grab a bird just leaving the ground.

The biological significance of another movement, often observed in the play of young cats, is less obvious, since its practical application is rarely seen. In a lightning upward movement of upturned pads and claws the kitten reaches under the plaything and throws it in a high arc over its own shoulder, to follow it immediately with a jump. Or, particularly with larger playthings, the kitten sits before the object, rears itself stiffly erect, reaches

underneath it with a paw from each side and throws it back over its head in a steeper and higher semi-circle. Frequently the animal follows the flying object with its eyes and pursues it with a high leap, landing where it fell. The practical purpose of these two series of movements is the catching of fish, the first series for smaller, the second for larger ones.

Still more interesting and aesthetically beautiful are the movements of kittens playing either together or with their mother. Their biological meaning is less easily explained than that of the prey-catching movements, since, when cats play together, instinctive movements, whose practical application extends to many different things, are performed in colourful confusion on one and the same object.

Behind the coal-box a kitten sits watching his brother who is seated in the middle of the kitchen floor unaware of this scrutiny. Like a bloodthirsty tiger the watcher quivers with anticipation, whips his tail to and fro, and describes the movements of head and tail which are performed also by adult cats. Its sudden spring belongs to the realm of an entirely different set of movements, designed not for preying but for the fight. Instead of leaping on its brother as on a prey—an action which may alternatively, of course, be performed—it assumes a threatening position while still galloping, arching its back and advancing broadsides on. The assaulted kitten likewise humps its back and the two stand thus for some time, with ruffled hair and sideways bent tails. As far as I know, this never takes place between adult cats. Each of the two kittens behaves rather as though the other were a dog, but nevertheless their game goes on like a genuine tom-cat fight. Clasping each other firmly with their fore-paws, they turn wild somersaults over and over each other, at the same time

moving their hind feet in a way which, in play with
a human being, can prove extremely painful.
Hugging its playmate in the iron grip of its fore-
paws, the kitten vigorously pushes both hind feet
with unsheathed claws against it, repulsing it with a
quick succession of kicks. In a genuine fight, these
slitting, tearing blows are directed at the unprotected
belly of an adversary where their action must be
devastating. After their short boxing match the
kittens release their hold of one another and now
an exciting chase usually follows, in which another
uncommonly graceful set of movements is seen.
When the fleeing kitten sees the other getting very
close, he suddenly turns a somersault which lands
him, with a soft and absolutely silent movement,
immediately underneath his pursuer. He digs his
fore-paws into its soft parts, scrabbling its face, at
the same time, with his hind feet.

How do these movements of play differ from those
of real earnest? In their form, even the most practised
eye may fail to detect a difference, but nevertheless
there is one. In these games, composed as they are
of the movements of catching a prey, fighting a
fellow cat, and repelling a foe, serious injury is never
done to the playmate acting one of these parts. The
social inhibition against real biting or deep scratch-
ing is fully enforced during play, while, in a case of
real earnest, it is obliterated by the emotion evoking
the particular series of movements. In serious situa-
tions, the animal is in a particular psychological
state which brings with it the readiness for a particular way of behaving—and for this way only. It is
typical of play, that, during it, highly specific behaviour is incited without the corresponding emotional state. The relationship of all play to play-
acting lies in the fact that the player 'pretends' to be

obsessed with an emotion which he does not really feel. In play, many separate sets of movements, serving many different biological ends, can be performed in irregular sequence because the particular emotional state which would elicit any one of them in a real emergency is lacking. The movements of fighting are enacted without anger, those of flight without fear, and those of preying without hunger or greed. It is not true that the emotions pertaining to the earnest situation are present in an attenuated form. In play, they are altogether missing, and the game is broken off immediately should any one of them suddenly swell up in either of the animals concerned. The urge to play arises from a different source, more general in nature than the individual drives which, in an emergency, supply every one of the described movements with specific energy.

But this general urge to play, the desire to indulge in vigorous action, for the mere joy of the thing, is a remarkable phenomenon only occurring in the mentally highest of all living creatures. Bridges has described it aptly from the poet's point of view,

> *I too will something make*
> *And joy in the making;*
> *Although to-morrow it seem*
> *Like empty words of a dream*
> *Remembered on waking.*

Not without reason does the sight of young animals at play touch our hearts, not without reason does play seem to us an activity to be more highly rated mentally than the corresponding actions performed in earnest, with their serious and species-preserving functions. Play differs from serious action not only in a negative sense, but in another positive respect. Play, especially in young animals, always has in it something of discovery. Play is typical of the developing organism; it regresses in the finished animal. I have called play 'Vor-Ahmung' (pre-imitation), an expression invented by Karl Groos, to indicate that the playful equivalents of certain, innate inherited movements occur in the life of an individual animal before their earnest application has begun. Groos attributes great educational value to play and contends that the different movements are perfected by frequent, playful repetition. We have good grounds for doubting this assertion in its general implication: instinctive, inherited movements mature like a bodily organ—they require no practice for their consummation as many observations can prove, and, in fact, we are shown by the perfect grace of movement exhibited by a kitten playing at 'mousing' or other games, that the movements as such neither require nor are capable of improvement.

Nevertheless, the kitten does learn from his play. He learns, not how to catch the mouse, but what a mouse is. In the first tentative advancement of a paw, in the first modest, hesitating angling movements after the ball of wool, lies a question: is this the object for which my dark senses long? which I can stalk, hunt, catch and finally devour? The inherited 'pattern' of prey, that is, the inherent mechanisms which elicit 'instinctive' prey-concerning movements, are fairly simple and not very comprehensive. Everything that is small, rounded and soft, everything that moves quickly by gliding or rolling, and, above all, everything that 'flees', evokes in the cat automatically and without previous experience the beautiful, elegant and 'cultivated' movements of 'mouse-catching'.

17. MAN AND THE CAT

Reposeful, patient, undemonstrative,
Luxurious, enigmatically sage,
Dispassionately cruel.

w. watson: *Study in Contrasts*

THERE are dog-lovers who cannot abide cats, and cat-lovers, particularly women, to whom dogs are anathema. In my opinion, both groups show pettiness: in fact, I consider it a proof of real love and understanding of animals only if a person is equally fond of the two creatures which of all animals stand nearest to us. To the genuine lover of nature, those qualities of the world of living things which most inspire his enthusiasm and reverence are the infinite variety they display and the innumerable ways in which nature produces fundamentally heterogeneous yet perfect harmonies.

From the standpoint of human psychology it is interesting to watch how various equally knowledgeable animal-lovers differ in their behaviour towards animals. They all wish to understand the animal better, whether purely for its own sake or for the sake of scientific research. Many naturalists desire to influence the animal as little as possible; they purposely avoid any personal contact with the creature

and behave like the field ornithologist or photographer who observes it from a well-concealed hiding place, his results depending upon the fact that the animals under observation are unconscious of his presence and behave accordingly. The opposite extreme is represented by the man who enters into a most intimate social contact with the animal, is treated by it as a member of its own species, and thus, in an entirely different way, penetrates the recesses of the mind of the species in question. Both of these two methods are justified, both have their advantages and disadvantages, and all imaginable transitions and combinations are possible. Which of the two methods should be adopted depends not only on the observer but also on the species he is examining: the higher its mental plane and the more social its nature the less he can dispense with personal contacts if he wishes really to understand it. Nobody can assess the mental qualities of a dog without having once possessed the love of one, and the same thing applies to many other intelligent socially living animals, such as ravens, jackdaws, large parrots, wild geese and monkeys.

With cats, the situation is a little different: while the greatest dog-lovers of my acquaintance are simultaneously the best connoisseurs of the species, I cannot say the same for cat-lovers. The mind of the cat is a delicate and wild thing, not easily disclosed to the type of person who forces his love obtrusively on an animal—a procedure to which dogs are more amenable. It is a fine test of real knowledge and understanding of animals and of nature how far the animal owner can desist from thrusting his love upon the object of his care. The cat is not a socially living animal; it is and remains an independent, wild, little panther, with nothing in its character of that infantility of domestication which makes the dog such a grateful recipient of attention and 'spoiling'. Now many passionate cat-lovers have no understanding of this feline need for independence. Over and over again, one hears the false contention that it is cruel to keep a large dog in a town flat but I have never heard the same said about cats. In reality the flat is merely a large kennel for a dog since he generally accompanies his master on walks and errands, but for the cat, it is nothing but a big cage. I do not mean that cats, particularly highly bred pedigree ones, suffer mentally from this confinement, but they certainly lose that quality of uncurbed wildness which, to me, constitutes their chief charm. I find it a constant source of wonder that I share my home with little tigers which are sometimes in and sometimes out, and which conduct their hunting expeditions and love affairs as though they still lived in their unhandled, pristine state in the wild woods. When, in the mornings, my big, tabby, half-Persian, Thomas II, used to stalk in majestically with leonine stride, his hair crusted with blood, his face gashed, and his already sorely-tried ear rent with a new wound, I would long to know who had been his adversary in the midnight duel and who the lady for whose favours they had fought. It always amazed me that the tame, affectionate creature, which sat on my knee purring contentedly in a deep bass, was the grim desperado whose wild, blood-curdling wails I had heard some hours ago, far away from the house.

The wide freedom which such a house-mate enjoys does not in any way minimize his dependence on man. In spite of their well-defined, wild, private lives which often kept them from home for days on end, my most temperamental and virile cats were, at the same time, the most affectionate of any that I have ever

known. Fawning, begging for food or sitting on somebody's knee and being stroked, are no indications of
real affection in any animal, least of all in a cat. The
question as to whether an animal sets any store by
the company of a certain person can only be
answered in one way: let that person take the animal
outside and allow it to decide spontaneously whether
it will remain with him or go its own way. The two
young cats, Thomas I and Thomas II, which I
reared myself, accepted me out of doors even when
they had reached maturity. Both greeted me with
that peculiar, ringing lip sound 'Frrrr' with which
adult cats express their true love, and both accompanied me on long walks in the surrounding woods.
On such excursions one must, of course, show some
consideration for the kind of paths which the cat
would choose if it were alone. One cannot expect it
to cross wide open spaces without trees or any cover
where it might fall prey to a passing dog, and one
must take the trouble to crawl through thick undergrowth and to adapt one's pace to that of the cat. At
first I used to be astonished how soon such a muscular
animal, physically fit and in the best of training, became tired and lagged behind. Which of all my
readers has ever seen a cat panting, with its tongue
hanging out of its mouth, like a dog? For most of us
a completely unfamiliar sight. A fully grown cat in
good health and strength is unable to follow the
leisurely pace of a strolling man even for half an hour
without showing signs of exhaustion. Therefore,
when walking with cats, one should not often make
such demands or they will soon tire of the pursuit.
However, if, in the choice of paths and in the pace
of one's stride, one accommodates oneself to one's
feline friend, one can make most interesting observations, particularly by letting him run ahead and then

following him bare-footed unobtrusively and silently. How much he sees, hears and smells which one would never have noticed without him! How infinitely cautious is his tread, ready at every step for instant flight! Unfortunately one never sees much of his hunting, for it only begins seriously at dusk.

following him bare-footed unobtrusively and silently. How much he sees, hears and smells which one would never have noticed without him! How infinitely cautious is his tread, ready at every step for instant flight! Unfortunately one never sees much of his hunting, for it only begins seriously at dusk.

I have owned many cats, particularly females, which indoors appeared much tamer than my two toms, but none of them took the slightest notice of me if we happened to meet outside. They simply 'cut' me and never greeted me with lip sounds, in fact they found it unequivocally vexatious and importunate of me if I attempted to join them, however unostentatiously I did it. This was in very marked contrast to the behaviour of Thomas II and his prolific wife, Pussy.

No wild animal—and the cat is a wild animal—can accord even the most trusted human being a higher degree of friendship than he would grant to a member of his own species under natural conditions. The fact that an adult tom-cat will accept a man as a companion in natural surroundings leads me to think that neither the domestic cat nor his wild forebear is nearly such a social recluse as is commonly supposed. Judging from my own experiences, the tom-cat is more able to form personal friendships than the female is, though my mother once possessed a feline couple, Dido and Aneas, both of whom used to accompany her on long walks through the woods.

It is certainly not my intention to dissuade anyone from keeping a cat in a town flat. The town-dweller has few enough contacts with nature and a handsome, unspoilt cat may well bring a touch of it into a city street, but I maintain that one can only appreciate the full charm of its being by giving the cat its freedom. My pleasantest feline memories are

those associated with quiet forest walks in the company of a tom-cat. And I maintain further that one can win, not the apparent, but the real love of a cat in no greater measure than by allowing it its natural way of living, and by seeking tactfully to approach it in its own natural surroundings. At the same time, one must accept the fact that the animal whose inmost wishes one thus respects is exposed to all the dangers which normally threaten such a small beast of prey. None of my cats died a natural death. Thomas I caught his paw in a trap and died of blood poisoning, and Thomas II fell a prey to his own passion for hunting: he stole several tame rabbits from a neighbouring farmer, who finally caught him red-handed and slew him on the spot. But it is in the nature of eagles, lions and tigers that they seldom meet with a peaceful end. And this is the essence of the cat as I love it, the inaccessible, unrestrained, wild animal. Strangely enough, this is also the very reason why the cat is so 'homely', for somebody or something can only be 'at home' whose profession lies outside; and the purring cat on the hearth betokens for me the symbol of homeliness just because he is not my prisoner but an independent being of almost equal status who happens to live in the same house that I do.

18. ANIMALS THAT LIE

IN another chapter of this book, I shall show how wrong it is to think that the cat, the proudest and most upright of our domestic animals, is 'deceitful'. At the same time, I do not regard this inability to deceive as a sign of the cat's superiority, in fact, I regard it as a sign of the much higher intelligence of the dog that it is able to do so. There is no doubt that clever dogs can dissemble up to a certain point and, in this chapter, I shall record some of my observations on this behaviour.

My old Bully was keenly aware of it if he had 'made a fool of himself' and herein he showed an extraordinary and inexplicable perception of a certain highly complicated social situation. There is no doubt that intelligent dogs know when they are cutting an undignified and, from a human point of view, comical figure. Many of them fly into a rage or become deeply depressed if they are laughed at on such occasions. In his excellent dog novel, *White Fang*, Jack London describes this behaviour which he has obviously witnessed himself. At the time of which I am writing, Bully was getting old and his eyesight was already failing; thus it often happened that he inadvertently barked at home-coming members of the family, myself included. He became painfully embarrassed when I tactfully overlooked his mistake and did not admonish him for it. But one day he did a thing which at first I took for coincidence but later recognized as a feat of great intelligence, namely a real and deliberate misrepresentation of facts. I had just opened the yard gate, and before I had had time to shut it the dog rushed up barking loudly. Upon recognizing me, he hesitated in a moment of acute embarrassment, then, pushing past my leg he raced through the open gates and across the lane where he continued to bark furiously at our neighbour's gate just as though he had been addressing an enemy in that garden from the very beginning. This time I believed him and concluded that I had imagined his moment of embarrassment and that I myself had made a wrong observation. Our neighbours really possessed a dog which was a rival of Bully's and his vituperations might easily have been addressed to it and not to me. However, his frequent, almost daily reiteration of this behaviour taught me that he had literally sought an excuse to veil the fact that he had accidentally barked at his master. Indeed, the moment of embarrassed hesitation when he suddenly recognized me became shorter and shorter with time; one might almost say he 'lied' more and more fluently. Now it often happened that, after the dog had recognized me and rushed past, he would arrive at a spot where there was nothing whatever to bark at, for instance in an empty corner of the yard. So he would just stand there barking furiously up at the wall.

One could account for this behaviour by attributing it to a physiological stimulus, but there is no doubt that his understanding was involved, for he made use of the same 'lie' for an entirely different kind of deception. Like all our dogs, Bully was forbidden to chase poultry and, though it infuriated him when our hens picked at the remains of his food, he did not dare to chase them or, to be more correct,

to admit that he was chasing them, but, with in-
dignant barks, he would rush into the middle of them
and make them scatter, wildly squawking. Then, instead of chasing one or snapping at it, he would run
straight on in the same direction, barking all the time,
just as he used to do when he had inadvertently barked
at me. And, in the same way, he often arrived at a
point where there was nothing within sight to bark
at. However this time he was not clever enough to
seek out a special object to bark at beyond the hens.

My present bitch, Susi, invented just the same
ruse when she was only seven months old. She
delights in scattering the wildly squawking hens by
jumping into the middle of them with loud barks and
then rushing down the garden barking uninterrupt-
edly. She returns remarkably quickly with an expression of complete innocence, and revealing her
not quite clear conscience by an ostentatious gesture
of affection—just like a little daughter.

My bitch Stasi practised a different kind of swindle.
It is well known that many dogs are not only
physically sensitive but that they love being pitied,
and are quick to learn how to influence a tender-
hearted person to their own advantage. During a
bicycle tour in Posen, a tendon of Stasi's left fore-paw
became inflamed as a result of overstrain. Since she
was extremely lame, I was obliged to walk with her
for some days instead of using the bicycle. Later on,
too, I was very careful of her and at once rode slowly
if I noticed that she was becoming tired or beginning
to limp. It did not take her long to realize this, and
if I rode in a direction uncongenial to her she very
soon went lame. If I cycled from my quarters to the
military hospital, where she might have to remain
on guard by my bicycle for hours on end, she limped
so pitifully that people in the road often reproached

me. But if we took the direction of the Army riding school where a cross-country ride was likely to ensue, the pain had gone. The swindle was most transparent on Saturdays. In the morning, on the way to duty, the poor dog was so lame that she could scarcely hobble behind the bicycle, but in the afternoon, when we covered the thirteen miles to the Ketscher See at a good speed, she did not run behind the bicycle but raced ahead of it at a gallop, along the paths which she knew so well. And on Monday she limped again. Finally, I should like to relate two little anecdotes which concern not dogs but apes, but which are relevant here, since they prove that the most intelligent animals can both tell lies and recognize them.

Professor Wolfgang Köhler, whose work on feats of intelligence in chimpanzees is world famous, once set a clever young male chimpanzee the well-known problem of reaching a bunch of bananas hanging from the ceiling, by pushing a large but light packing case from another corner of the room and standing on it. The animal took stock of the situation then turned not to the case but to the professor, whom it took by the hand. Now chimpanzees have an uncommonly expressive way of directing attention by nods and looks, and they will show another chimpanzee or a human friend where they want him to go by means of begging tones and hand pulling. Using such looks and gestures, the monkey attempted to lead Prof. Köhler to something in another corner of the room. The professor followed the pressing demands of the animal, for he was curious to know what it wished to draw his attention to. He did not notice that he was being led exactly under the bananas, nor did he realize its true intentions till it suddenly clambered up him as if he were a tree and, pushing

off vigorously from his head, seized the bananas and fled with them. The monkey's solution of the problem was different from but cleverer than the one expected of him.

The counterpart of this story of the chimpanzee which lied to the famous psychologist is that of the orang-utan which was lied to by my friend, J. Portielje, the director of the Amsterdam Zoo. It was an enormous male Sumatra orang-utan, captured as an adult, which lived in a very roomy and very high cage. In order to provide exercise for the animal which, like all orang-utans, was somewhat lazy, Portielje had instructed the keepers to give it a little food at a time at the very top of the cage, so that it was forced to make a short climbing tour every time it wanted a piece of banana. With orang-utans, it is apparently necessary to imitate in this way the difficulties of the natural struggle for existence and to force the animals to take a certain amount of more lively exercise; perhaps the psychological effect of this natural 'work' is more important than the physical one. The animal's habit of going to the top of the cage for food was also made use of by the keepers when the cage needed cleaning. While one keeper kept the ape occupied with food near the roof, another one quickly cleaned the wooden floor with broom and bucket. On one occasion this rather risky procedure might have had serious consequences if Portielje had shown less presence of mind. While one of the keepers was cleaning the floor, the orang-utan suddenly came sliding down the cage bars, and, before the sliding door could be pushed into its lock, the huge creature had inserted its powerful hands between the door and the post. Although both Portielje and the keeper exerted all their strength in the attempt to close it, the orang-utan pulled it slowly but surely back, inch by inch. When it was just open enough for the animal to escape, Portielje was struck by a bright idea, such as can only occur to a past master of animal psychology; he suddenly released the door and, jumping back with a loud cry, gazed, as though horrified, at a point immediately behind the orang. The animal spun round in an instant to see what was going on behind it and in the same moment the door snapped in the lock. A few seconds passed before it realized that it had been tricked by a false alarm, but when this dawned on the animal it worked itself up into such a frenzy of rage that it would certainly have torn the man to pieces if the door had not been safely bolted. There was no doubt that it understood that it had been the victim of a premeditated falsehood.

19. 'CAT!'

Macavity, Macavity, there is no one like Macavity.
There never was a cat of such deceitfulness and suavity.

                                                    T. S. ELIOT

THE epithet 'Catty!' generally implies deceitfulness in the person (usually of feminine
gender) against whom it is directed. I have often
wondered why the cat has earned this reputation. It
cannot be the way it hunts—silently, stalking its
prey, for it is well known that lions and tigers hunt
in exactly the same way, but nobody would dream
of saying, 'Lioness!' or 'Tigress!' to a malicious
woman who gossips about her neighbours. Conversely, the term 'bloodthirsty' is applied to lions
and tigers, though never to our domestic cat although
it, too, bites its prey to death.

In the chapter, 'Animals that Lie', I have re-
counted everything I know about real deceitfulness,
that is, conscious dissembling, in animals, and I consider this behaviour a tremendous and almost incredible feat of animal intelligence. Some of my
colleagues will probably question the few examples
I have given and may consider them too few to justify
my assumption that the animals in question were
consciously swindling. I have never seen an analogous case of duplicity in a cat, although I have

lived with these animals nearly as long and as intimately as with dogs, nor do I know of any typical
behaviour of cats which could foster even the erron-
eous notion that they are deceitful. In several other
species of animals I do know of behaviour which
would give to an experienced observer the impression
of calculated deceit, although, in reality, nothing of
the kind is involved.

Some dogs are so shy that they will not, I will even
say cannot, allow strangers to touch them. Such dogs
frequently assume a cringing attitude, and therein
lies the difficulty, for they often wag their tails deferentially. Only a knowledgeable observer will notice
that the dog is trying to avoid the human touch, and
crouches lower and lower beneath the hand which
for some reason unknown to the animal is trying to
stroke it. Should the tactlessly importunate human
being persist in his attentions and actually touch the
dog, the terrified animal may lose control of itself and
snap like lightning and with punishing severity at the
offending hand. A considerable number of dog-bites
are attributable to this kind of *Angstbeissen* ('biting
from fear'). The victim of this surprise attack blames
the dog all the more for having first of all wagged
its tail.

The behaviour of bears may be misunderstood in a
slightly different way, and, as a result, these animals
may be branded as deceitful. Bears are solitary animals, their 'interbear' social relations are at a low
stage of development and they are rather expression-
less. The thick skin of their faces is poorly furnished
with the muscles of expression, and their small, prick
ears, set deep in the thick fur of their heads, are little
exposed to danger while fighting: an angry bear hits
out suddenly with a lightning movement of its paw,
but it does not snap suddenly with its teeth; thus it

is one of the few large mammals which does not lay back its ears in rage. Since its other expressions are also rather inconspicuous, and particularly because they do not resemble those of the dog, a human being often does not notice when a bear is angry, until it is too late. Moreover, tame bears in particular are prone to sudden and unpredictable outbreaks of fury. The rounded proportions and comically cheerful deportment of a healthy bear show an outward resemblance to a certain type of good-tempered man, and one is instinctively unable to expect a sudden outburst of rage from such a cheerful, fat and homely creature. The American Zoo Director, Hornaday, one of the best informed authorities on bears and their behaviour, describes tame bears as the most dangerous of all animals kept in captivity. 'If thine enemy offend thee, give him a tame, young bear,' is his philanthropic advice. In his charming book, *The Mind and Manners of Wild Animals*, Hornaday describes some truly terrible mishaps with tame bears, some of which occurred with very young animals. The bear, which, with pricked ears and unbared fangs, calmly eats an apple out of its owner's hand and in the very next moment lands him a blow on the head with its iron-hard claws, seems to be false and cunning, and Hornaday's remark that the bear always lives behind a mask is understandable. Nevertheless, this judgment is neither true nor fair, inasmuch as the bear does not purposely dissemble. It is not its fault that, as a solitary and unsocial animal, it simply lacks the expressive movements with which other, more social animals announce their inner feelings to fellow members of their species.

In the reputedly 'catty' cat, these expressive movements are particularly highly developed. There are few animals in whose faces a knowledgeable

observer can so clearly read a prevailing mood and predict what actions—friendly or hostile—are likely to follow. The face of the cat portrays so clearly and unmistakably the slightest degree of mental agitation that anybody who is familiar with this animal knows at once how he stands with it. How plain is the expression of trustful friendliness when, with erect ears and wide open eyes, a cat turns a smooth unwrinkled face towards its observer, and how clearly expressed by the facial musculature is every rising emotion, whether of fear or of hostility. The striped markings in the face of the 'wild-coloured' cat enhance the least movements of the facial skin and augment the vividness of the expression. This is one of the reasons why I prefer the wild-coloured, 'tiger' domestic cat to all others. The slightest vestige of mistrust—which does not yet border on fear—and the innocent round eyes become somewhat almond shaped and oblique, and the ears less erect; and it requires neither the subtle change of bodily attitude nor the gently waving tip of the tail to inform the observer that the mental state of the animal is undergoing a transition.

The threatening attitudes of a cat are extraordinarily expressive, and are entirely different in their manifestation according to whom they are directed against: whether they apply to a human friend who has 'gone too far', or to a feared enemy, perhaps a dog or another cat. They are different too, according to whether they are made purely in self-defence or whether they imply self-assurance in the animal and predict a forthcoming attack. Cats always announce their intention of attacking, and, except in the case of unreliable or mentally deficient psychopaths—which occur in cats just as in dogs— they never bite or scratch without giving previous unmistakable warning to the offender. Usually, indeed, the gradually increasing threatening gestures are suddenly exaggerated just before action is taken; this is evidently an ultimatum, 'If you don't leave me alone at once, I shall unfortunately be obliged to take reprisals.'

The cat threatens dogs—or any other dangerous preying animals—by making its well-known 'hunch back'. Standing on straight, stiff legs and making itself as tall as possible, it ruffles the hair of back and tail holding the latter slightly to one side in order to make its whole dimensions appear larger to the enemy, almost as some fishes do in self-display or to intimidate a foe. The cat's ears are laid flat, the corners of its mouth are pulled backwards, and the nose is wrinkled. From its chest a low, strangely metallic growl issues, which culminates now and again in the well-known 'spitting', that is, a forced expiration during which the throat is wide open and the incisors exposed. In itself, this threatening gesture is doubtless meant to be defensive; it is most frequently seen when a cat suddenly finds itself face to face with a big dog and has no time to withdraw. Should the dog come nearer in spite of this warning, the cat does not flee but attacks as soon as the dog has overstepped a certain, definite 'critical distance'. It hurls itself at the dog's face and, with claws and teeth, savages its most sensitive places, if possible the eyes and nose. Should the dog show the least sign of flinching, the cat regularly makes use of this slight breathing space to take flight. Thus the short feline attack is only to gain time while finding a way of escape. There is, however, one contingency in which a cat may make a prolonged and earnest attack in this hunch-backed attitude, and that is when she is defending her young. In this case, she approaches her enemy when he is some distance away and she moves

in a peculiar fashion, galloping with an up and down and sideways motion, for she must continually present her imposing broadside to the foe. Though this broadsides gallop with laterally held tail is seldom to be seen in real earnest, it can very often be observed in the play of young cats. I have never seen it in mature tom-cats, except in play, for there is no situation in which they are obliged to attack an enemy like this. In the suckling female cat, this broadsides attack brings with it an absolute and unconditional readiness for self-sacrifice, and, in this state, even the gentlest cat is almost invincible. I have seen large dogs, notorious cat killers, capitulate and flee before such an attack. Ernest Seton Thompson graphically describes a charming and doubtless true occurrence, in which a mother cat in Yellowstone Park put a bear to flight and pursued him until he climbed a tree in terror.

The threatening which precedes a battle between two cats, particularly males, is entirely different, but just as impressive and magnificent to watch. The animals stand opposed to one another stiff-legged as before, but in this case, the hunched back and broadsides attitude are almost entirely in abeyance. The threatening toms stand head to head, growling and screaming in their too familiar tones, and swishing their tails. Apart from this movement, they stand like statues for an amazingly long time, up to many minutes. Each tries to break down the morale of the other, on the principle of 'who can stick it out the longest'. All other movements, particularly the advancing of the dominant cat, are carried out in slow motion. Slowly, very slowly, one animal moves forward by a fraction of an inch, screaming horrible threats into the face of the other, and it may be a long time before hostilities break out like an explosion, quickly as lightning, which the human eye can scarcely follow. In *Wild Animals I have Known* Ernest Seton Thompson has described the tom-cat fight in all its complicated ceremonial, so vividly that I decline to do it here again—an imitation would be inevitable.

Another type of threatening, associated not with self-display but with gestures of humiliation, is seen when a cat is 'teased' to the limits of endurance by a friendly human being. This type of inhibited threatening, which is accompanied by supplicating gestures of humiliation, is most commonly seen at cat shows or other such institutions, where the animals are in strange surroundings and must submit to being touched by judges and other people whom they do not know. A cat thus frightened shrinks down, making itself lower and lower until its body is flat against the floor. Its ears are laid back threateningly and the tip of its tail moves angrily from side to side. If it is very wrought up it may begin to growl in an undertone. In this mood it seeks cover at any price and will dash behind a cupboard, the pipes of a central heating or—a favourite place for feline patients in veterinary surgeries—up the chimney. If no such cover is at hand it will press its back against the wall, lying half on one side. It will also take up this half sideways position on the judging table at a cat show; it portends the readiness to hit out with a fore-paw. The more frightened the animal becomes, the more sideways becomes its position, until finally one paw is raised from the ground and the claws are unsheathed for action. Should the fear of the cat mount still higher, this reaction leads to the last desperate means of defence which the animal has at its disposal: it rolls right over on to its back and turns all its weapons towards its aggressor.

This last behaviour is often seen during judging at cat shows, and even knowledgeable cat owners are constantly surprised how little notice an experienced judge takes of this dangerous looking threatening of the small beast of prey and how complacently he touches the animal which, with paw raised to hit, is singing from a widely opened throat the up and down melody of the tom-cat song. Although the cat is saying unmistakably, 'Don't touch me or I will bite and scratch in earnest!', at the critical moment it doesn't really do it, or, at the most, it only does it very half-heartedly. For the acquired inhibitions of the 'good', tamed animal can stand up even to this sore trial. Thus the cat does not feign friendliness and then scratch and bite but, on the contrary, it threatens to rid itself of the (from a feline point of view) insufferable attentions of the judge, but cannot bring itself to put its threat into action.

I am therefore really unable to discover what is 'catty' about a cat, than which no animal shows its feelings more clearly. The only explanation that I can find for the undeserved reputation of our domestic cat is one which is not flattering to human beings, or at any rate to the human female. Even the non-anthropomorphizing observer, who fully appreciates the masculinity of a virile tom-cat, must admit that the soft grace of movement which is so typical of cats and of all feline beasts of prey, bears an undoubted resemblance to the grace of women, in particular women of a certain type. But this type of woman—and herein lies my point—is quite inscrutable to us poor men but, at the same time attractive and therefore dangerous! It is this type of woman, of which Carmen is the purest representative, who has earned for herself all the masculine complaints of falseness with which the world's literature is furnished, and I sincerely believe that the cat is looked upon as false and 'catty' because many similarly graceful women really deserve those epithets.

20. THE ANIMAL WITH A CONSCIENCE

The guilt of conscience take thou for thy labour
SHAKESPEARE: *Richard II*

LIVING in the natural environment which has influenced its gradual development throughout the earth's history, the wild animal enjoys in a certain sense the paradise that man has lost. Every single urge which wells up in a wild animal is 'good', that is, all instinctive impulses from an inner source are such that they must finally contribute to the good of the particular animal and of its whole species. For a wild animal in its natural state, there is no conflict between natural inclinations and what they 'ought' to do, and this is the paradise which man has lost. The fruits of man's higher mental capacities are his cultural development, and above all, the power of speech and of conceptual thought, and the accumulation and traditional passing on of common knowledge. All this has resulted in man's historical evolution at a rate which is many hundreds of times more rapid than the purely organic genealogical development of all other living beings. But the instincts, the innate actions and reactions of man, remain tied to the much slower rate of organic development and are unable to keep pace with his cultural development.

'Natural inclinations' no longer quite fit in with conditions of human culture, where they have been largely superseded by human intellect. Man is not 'bad' from birth onwards, but he is not good enough for the demands of cultivated society which he has imposed upon himself. In contrast to the wild animal, the cultivated human being—and in this sense every human being is cultivated—can no longer rely blindly on his instincts: many of these are so obviously opposed to the demands made by society on the individual that even the most naive person must realize that they are anti-cultural and anti-social.

The voice of instinct, which the wild animal can obey unrestrainedly since it always speaks for the good of the individual and of the species, has become, for man, very often a destructive whispering, the more dangerous since it speaks the same language as other impulses which he not only should but must obey. Therefore man is forced to test, with the help of conscious thought, every single impulse and to ask himself if he may yield to it without damaging the cultural values which he has created. It was the fruits of the tree of knowledge that compelled man to relinquish a safe, animal, instinctive existence in a fixed, narrow environment, but they also enable him to extend his environment to world-wide dimensions, and to put himself the responsible question: may I yield to the impulse within me or will I, by doing so, imperil the highest values of our human society? Above all, it is conscious thought which has forced us to the unavoidable realization that as members of human society we are but parts of a whole, and from this knowledge of our membership of society conscience has sprung and faces us with the inevitable question: what would happen if I did everything to which my inner impulses are urging

me at this moment? This is the biological version of Kant's teaching on the categorical question: can I raise the maxims of my actions to the level of a general law of nature or would the result be opposed to reason?

True morality, in the highest human sense of the word, presupposes a mental capacity which no animal possesses, and conversely, human responsibility would itself be impossible without a definite foundation of sentiment. Even in man, the feeling of responsibility has its roots in the deep, instinctive 'layers' of his mind and he may not do with impunity all that cold reason affirms. While ethical motives may amply justify a certain action, inner feeling may rebel against it, and woe betide the man who in such a case listens to reason rather than to sentiment. In this connection, I shall tell a little story. Many years ago, in the Zoological Institute, I had under my care a number of young giant snakes which lived on dead mice and rats. The proper meal for a young python was a fully grown mouse, and twice a week I used to kill a mouse for each of the six snakes which ate it quite tamely out of my hand. Now mice are more difficult to breed than rats, so the institute possessed a much larger number of the latter. It would have been all right to feed the snakes on rats but then I should have been obliged to kill the young ones, and baby rats of mouse size are the most charming little creatures, with their plump heads, their big eyes, their short fat legs and babyishly clumsy movements. I was therefore loth to use them as food, and it was only when I had reduced the mouse supply of the institute to a fraction of its former state and thus evoked the ire of the animal breeding department that I decided to resort to the baby rats. I hardened my heart by asking myself

whether I was an experimental zoologist or a sentimental old spinster, killed six young rats and fed
them to my charges. From the point of view of
Kantian ethics this deed was absolutely justifiable,
for reason tells us that it is no more reprehensible to
kill young rats than old mice. But all that is of no
account to the deep feelings in the inmost recesses
of the human soul, and this time I had to pay dearly
for hearkening to reason and allowing it to overcome
the inhibitions of sentiment which strove to prevent
my committing that infanticide. Every night for at
least a week I dreamed of it. Every night I was
forced to repeat the slaughter. In my dreams the baby
rats appeared much more appealing and tender than
they really are: they assumed the features of human
babies, cried with human voices and refused to die
as often as I banged their heads against the floor—
the quickest and most painless way of killing small
animals of this kind. I will not depict further all the
horrors of those dreams which were painted with the
infernal phantasy of a Brueghel. There is no doubt
that the damage I incurred by killing those baby
rats bordered on a slight neurosis. Anyway, I have
learnt a lesson by it and have never since been
ashamed of being sentimental and of listening to my
inmost feelings, however reasonable a categorical
imperative bids me ignore them. For this reason I am
incapable of performing research which involves
vivisection, although from a moral point of view I
certainly cannot condemn it wholesale. When I consider the extent of the mental injury I inflicted on
myself by killing six little baby rats, it is easy to
imagine what a person experiences who, even from
the highest ethical motives, breaks down the inhibitions which restrain a normal human being from
killing another one. If even those dead young rats

haunted my dreams for several nights, one can well realize how his crime pursues the human murderer in a way which makes Poe's story of *The Tell-tale Heart* seem quite credible.

This form of remorse, which is deeply rooted in the emotions, has a counterpart in the mentality of highly developed, social animals, and I have often observed a type of behaviour in dogs which has led me to draw this conclusion. I have already described my French bulldog, Bully. He was old but still very temperamental when on a ski-ing tour, I acquired the Hanoverian Schweisshund, or rather, he acquired me, since he insisted forcibly on accompanying me to Vienna. His arrival was a hard blow for poor Bully, and had I known how much the old dog was going to suffer from jealousy I should probably not have brought the handsome Hirschmann home. For days the atmosphere was heavy with tension which finally discharged itself in one of the most embittered dog-fights that I have ever witnessed, and the only one which ever took place in the master's room where normally even sworn enemies observed a cease-fire. Whilst I was separating the combatants, Bully accidentally bit me deep in the ball of the right little finger. That was the end of the fight, but poor Bully had incurred the severest shock to the nervous system that a dog can ever receive: he broke down completely and although I did not admonish him and indeed stroked and coaxed him, he lay on the carpet as though paralysed, a little bundle of unhappiness, unable to get up. He shivered as in a fever and every few seconds a great tremor ran through his body. His breathing was quite superficial but from time to time a deep sigh escaped his tortured breast, and large tears overflowed his eyes. As he was literally unable to rise, I had to carry him down on to the road several times a day; he then walked back himself, but the nervous shock had so reduced the tone of his muscles that he could only crawl upstairs with an effort. Anyone who saw the dog at that time without knowing the previous history must have imagined him to be severely ill. It was several more days before he would eat and even then he could only be cajoled into taking food from my hands. For many weeks he approached me in an attitude of humble supplication, in sad contrast to the normal behaviour of this self-willed and anything but servile dog. His bad conscience affected me the more in that my own was anything but clear towards him. My acquisition of the new dog now seemed an almost unforgivable act.

I once had an equally moving if less heart-rending experience with a male English bulldog which belonged to a neighbouring family in Altenberg. Bonzo, as the dog was called, was savage with strangers but docile towards friends of the family, and he not only knew me well but would greet me politely and even enthusiastically whenever our paths happened to cross. I was once invited to tea at Schloss Altenberg, the home of Bonzo and his mistress. I drew up on my motor-cycle in front of the house which occupies a lonely position in the forest. I had dismounted and, with my back to the door, was bending down to adjust the stand of the machine, when Bonzo shot out and, quite understandably failing to recognize my overall-clad backside, seized my leg in his teeth and hung on in true bulldog style. I yelled out his name in agonized tones, whereupon he fell as though shot by a gun and grovelled before me on the ground. As there had obviously been a misunderstanding and as in any case my thick outfit had prevented serious injury—a few bruises on the shin-bone do not matter to a motor-cyclist—I spoke encouragingly to Bonzo,

caressed him and was ready to forget it. But not so the bulldog: the whole afternoon he followed me round and at tea he leaned against my leg. Every time I looked at him he sat up very straight, fixed on me his protruding bulldog eyes and pleaded forgiveness by frantically offering his paw. When we met in the road some days later, he did not greet me in his usual boisterous fashion but in the same attitude of humility, giving me his paw which I shook heartily.

When assessing the behaviour of these two dogs, one must realize that neither of them had ever bitten either me or anybody else, and had consequently never been punished for an offence of this kind. How then could they know that what they had done, quite inadvertently, came under the category of crime? I believe that they were in the same state of mind as I was myself after I had killed those young rats: they had done something which an inhibition, deeply rooted in their instinctive feelings, forbade them to do, and the fact that the crime was committed by accident and was therefore excusable from the standpoint of moral reason no more prevented a pysychological shock to the perpetrator than did my logical arguments in vindication of the rat-killing.

An entirely different kind of bad conscience is that of intelligent dogs who have done something which from the standpoint of their innate social inhibitions is natural and permissible, but which is forbidden by an acquired 'Taboo', the result of careful training. The expression of false innocence and exaggerated virtue with which clever dogs—like children—know how to mask their features on such occasions is known to every dog lover, who can assume with certainty that it hides a guilty conscience. So quaintly humanlike is this behaviour that it is often difficult for the castigator to mete out the necessary penalty. I myself find it equally hard to chastise a dog for a first offence committed with a clear conscience and without any expectation of punishment.

Wolf I, one of the older generation of my cross-bred Chow-Alsatians, was a most bloodthirsty hunter but was nevertheless absolutely reliable with poultry as long as he realized that it belonged to me. But with new acquisitions which were strange to him he gave us a few unpleasant surprises. One Christmas my wife gave me four half-grown peacocks, and before it had occurred to us to fear for them Wolf had broken down the door of their pen and already killed one before I appeared on the scene. He was punished for it and from that day forth he never so much as looked at any of the remaining birds. These peacocks were the first gallinaceous birds that we had so far kept in this dog's lifetime and they obviously did not enter into his conception of the inviolable.

His inhibitions against killing different breeds of birds threw an interesting light on the ability of the dog to distinguish between them, almost, one might say, to view them in the abstract. All ducks were to him invulnerable; even in the case of those breeds which diverged widely from the normal he did not have to be told that they were under the protection of the law. Since he had been taught not to kill peacocks, I assumed that from now on he would respect all gallinaceous birds just as he respected ducks, but I was wrong, for when I got some bantam Wyandottes for hatching out duck eggs, Wolf again broke into the same pen and killed all seven, without, however, eating a single one. Again he was chastised—a mild punishment sufficed, it being really enough to point out to him what was forbidden—and new hens were obtained, against which he never sinned again. When, a few months later, I received some gold and silver pheasants, I had become wiser. I called the dog up to the crates, pushed his nose gently against the pheasants and gave him a few light slaps, uttering threatening words as I did so. This prophylactic treatment amply fulfilled its purpose: Wolf never touched one of them. On the other hand, he did something very interesting in the light of animal psychology; one fine spring morning, I came into the garden and, to my horror and astonishment, saw Wolf standing in the middle of the lawn with a pheasant in his mouth. He did not hear me so I was able to watch him undisturbed. Curiously enough, he neither shook the bird nor maltreated it in any other way but just stood quite quietly looking rather bewildered. When I called him he evinced no sign of a bad conscience but, evidently welcoming my signal, came trotting towards me with tail on high and the bird still in his mouth. Then I saw that it was a wild pheasant and not one of our tame gold or silver ones. Apparently the highly intelligent dog had been searching his conscience as to whether the bird trespassing in our garden belonged to the 'untouchables' or not. Obviously he had taken it at first for normal game and caught it, but then, for perhaps the scent reminded him of the forbidden birds, desisted from killing it as he would at once have done any other quarry. He was therefore quite prepared and indeed relieved to leave the decision to me. The magnificent cock pheasant, which was quite uninjured, lived for many years in one of our aviaries and later produced young with one of our hand-reared hens.

The Altenberg research animals were all treated so respectfully by our large and savage dogs that they hardly realized the risks they ran from them. One could teach the dogs that they must not hurt the geese but it was quite impossible to impress upon the geese that they must leave the dogs alone. The redoubtable grey-lag ganders attributed it no doubt to their own fighting prowess that the dogs shunned them meticulously in order to avoid a conflict. The fearlessness of the wild geese was astonishing and one cold winter's day I watched the following scene: three big dogs raced down the garden to the fence adjoining the road, intending to bark at some enemy. In the middle of their 'line of barking' lay a tightly huddled little group of six wild geese which the dogs, barking all the time, sprang clean over. None of the geese made the slightest move to get up, only a few necks stretched hissing in the direction of the dogs. On the way back, the dogs preferred to leave the trodden path and describe a wide semicircle in the deep snow around those shy wild fowl.

One old gander, the despot of the colony, seemed to imagine that teasing the dogs was his special calling in life. His wife was sitting on eggs near a short flight of steps which leads from our garden to the yard and the entrance gate. Since it was one of the self-imposed but steadily observed duties of the dogs to bark at that gate every time it was opened, they had to go up and down the steps very often. The old wild gander soon found that by ensconcing himself on the top step he could seize heaven-sent opportunities of pestering the dogs and of tweaking one of their tails every time they swept by. The only way they could reach the gate was by whizzing past this hissing Cerberus with their tails tucked tightly between their legs. The good-natured and rather sensitive Bubi, my father's dog, the son of my bitch Tito, grandfather of the above mentioned Wolf I, and great, great, great, great, great grandfather of my

present bitch, Susi, suffered much from the aggressions of the gander, for, of our three dogs, he was the most frequently attacked. He used to let out a premonitory yelp of pain every time he got ready to cross that fatal step. This impossible state of affairs found a dramatic and tragi-comic end. One fine day the bad old gander lay dead at his post. The autopsy revealed a minimal fracture of the base of the skull, evidently caused by the light impression of a dog's tooth. And Bubi was missing. He did not appear at feeding time and, after a careful search had been made, he was finally discovered, in a state of complete nervous breakdown, in a dark corner of the wash-house loft, wedged between some old packing cases, a place never normally frequented by our dogs. What had happened was as clear to me as if I had seen it take place: the old gander had seized the rushing Bubi so firmly by the tail that the dog had been unable to resist making a snap of self-defence at the seat of the pain. In doing so he had unfortunately nipped the gander in such a way that one of his incisors had indented the old gentleman's skull, and the injury had probably only proved fatal because the bones of the ancient bird, which was in its 25th year, were already brittle with age. Bubi was not punished. He was exonerated through extenuating circumstances and the peculiar physical condition of the victim. The latter was destined for the Sunday table, where it helped to shatter the widespread superstition that old wild geese must of necessity be tough. The big, fat gander tasted excellent and made a most palatable meal. My wife wondered whether old geese start getting tender again after the twentieth year.

21. FIDELITY AND DEATH

*This thought is as a death, which cannot choose
But weep to have that which it fears to lose.*

SHAKESPEARE: *Sonnets*

WHEN God created the world, He evidently
did not foresee the future bond of friendship
between man and the dog, or perhaps He had definite
and, to us, inexplicable reasons for assigning to the
dog a span of life five times shorter than that of his
master. In human life there is enough suffering—of
which everybody gets his share—when we come to
take leave of someone we love, and when we see the
end approaching, inevitably predestined by the fact
that he was born a few decades earlier than ourselves
we may well ask ourselves whether we do right to
hang our hearts on a creature which will be overtaken by senility and death before a human being,
born on exactly the same day, has even passed his
childhood; for it is a sad reminder of the transience
of earthly life when the dog, which a few years ago—
and it seems but a few months—was a clumsy cuddle-
some pup, begins to show unmistakable signs of age
and we know that his end must be expected in some
two or three years. I must admit that the ageing of a
dearly loved dog has always depressed me and at
times considerably enhanced the gloom which occasionally afflicts every man when he thinks of griefs to

come. Then there is the severe mental conflict which every master has to undergo when his dog is finally stricken in old age with some incurable disease, and the fatal question arises whether and when one should have him painlessly destroyed. Strangely enough fate has so far spared me this decision, since, with one exception, all my dogs have died a sudden and painless death at a ripe old age and without any intervention on my part. But one cannot count on this and I do not altogether blame sensitive people who shrink from acquiring a dog in view of the final inevitable parting. Not altogether blame them? Well, actually, I suppose I do. In human life all pleasures must be paid for by sorrow, for, as Burns says,

> *Pleasures are like poppies spread,*
> *You seize the flower, its bloom is shed;*
> *Or like the snow falls in the river*
> *A moment white—then melts for ever;*

and fundamentally I consider the man a shirker who renounces the few permissible and ethically irreproachable pleasures of life for fear of having to pay the bill with which, sooner or later, fate will present him. He who is miserly with the coin of suffering had better retire to some spinsterly attic and there gradually desiccate like a sterile bulb which bears no blossoms. Certainly the death of a faithful dog which has accompanied its master for some fifteen years of his life's walk brings with it much suffering, nearly as much as the death of a beloved person. But in one essential detail the former is easier to bear: the place which the human friend filled in your life remains for ever empty, that of your dog can be filled with a substitute. Dogs are indeed individuals, personalities in the truest sense of the words and I should be

the last to deny this fact, but they are much more like
each other than are human beings. The individual
differences between living creatures are in direct
proportion to their mental development: two fishes
of one species are, in all their actions and reactions,
practically the same; but, for a person familiar with
their behaviour, two golden hamsters or jackdaws
show noticeable diversities; two hooded crows or
two grey-lag geese are sometimes quite separate
individuals.

In dogs this holds good to a still greater extent, since
they, as domestic animals exhibit in their behaviour
an immeasurably greater amount of individual variation than those other non-domesticated species. But,
conversely, in the depths of their soul, in those deep
instinctive feelings which are responsible for their
special relationship with man, dogs resemble each
other closely, and if on the death of one's dog one
immediately adopts a puppy of the same breed, one
will generally find that he refills those spaces in one's
heart and one's life which the departure of an old
friend has left desolate. Under certain conditions the
consolation thus afforded can be so thorough that
one feels almost ashamed of one's unfaithfulness to
one's former dog. Here again, the dog is more faithful
than his master, for had the master died the dog
would scarcely have found a substitute within the
space of half a year. These considerations will perhaps seem absurd to people who will not admit of
any moral responsibility towards an animal but
they have prompted me to an unusual course of
action.

When one day, I found my old Bully lying dead of
a stroke on his old accustomed 'barking beat', I at
once regretted deeply that he had left no successor to
take his place. I was then 17 years old and this was

the first time I had lost a dog; I am unable to express how much I missed him. He had been my inseparable companion for years and the limping rhythm of his trot when he ran behind me—he was lame from a badly healed broken fore-leg—had become so much the sound of my own footsteps that I no longer heard his rather weighty tread and the snuffing that accompanied it. I only noticed it when it was no longer there. In the weeks that immediately followed Bully's death, I really began to understand what it is that makes naïve people believe in the ghosts of their dead. The constant sound throughout years of the dog trotting at my heels had left such a lasting impression on my brain—psychologists call this an 'eioletic' phenomenon—that for weeks afterwards, as if with my own ears, I heard him pattering after me.

On quiet Danube paths this reached the pitch of an almost sinister hallucination. If I listened consciously the trotting and snuffing ceased at once, but as soon as my thoughts began to wander again I seemed to hear it once more. It was only when Tito, at that time still a wobbly half-grown puppy, began to run behind me that the spectre of Bully, the limping ghost dog, was finally banished.

Tito too died long ago, and how long ago! But her spirit still trots sniffing at my heels. I have taken good care that it should do so, by resorting to a peculiar course of action: when Tito lay dead before me, just as unexpectedly as Bully had done, I realized that another dog would take her place just as she had taken Bully's, and, feeling ashamed of my own faithlessness, I swore a strange pledge to her memory: henceforward only Tito's descendants should accompany me through life. A man cannot keep faith with an individual dog for obvious biological reasons, but he can remain true to the breed. The dog is much nearer than man to nature, whose relentlessness Tennyson so aptly sums up with the words,

> *So careful of the type she seems,*
> *So careless of the single life.*

Even in mankind, with our exaggerated individualities, the type is preserved in a remarkable way by heredity. When my little daughter, in a moment of embarrassment, throws back her head with the peculiarly arrogant movement which was typical of my mother, whom the child has never seen; when she and likewise her brother under stress of deep thought wrinkle their brows just as my wife's father used to do, what is this but 'reincarnation' in the most literal sense of the word? I have always had a particularly sharp eye for expressive movements and it is this faculty which has destined me for the work of animal observation. Owing to these acute powers of mine, I am always deeply moved by those expressive movements of my children which, years before their birth, I had noticed in their grandparents. These movements are, after all, the outward and visible signs of deeply rooted, immutable properties of soul, good and bad, desirable and dangerous. I often find it uncanny—as the ghosts of the dead are to the living—when I observe how, in one of my children, the character traits of all four grandparents crop up one after the other, or sometimes all at once. If I had known their great grandparents, I should probably see them too in my children and might even discover them strangely jumbled and divided amongst my children's children.

I am constantly stimulated to such reflections on death and immortality by the apparently innocent and uncomplicated personality of my little bitch

Susi, nearly all of whose forebears I knew, since in
our stud a certain amount of unavoidable and permissible inbreeding was practised. Just as the personal character traits of a dog are incomparably
simpler than those of a man and are thus correspondingly more obvious when encountered in combination in an individual descendant, so every reappear-
ance of the character traits of their progenitors is
immeasurably more patent than in man. In animals,
where the inherited is much less overshadowed by
the individually acquired than in man, the spirit of
their ancestors takes more immediate possession
of the living, where the character propensities of
the dead find more unmistakable living expression.

When, hypocritically, I assure a guest who inter-
rupts my work that he is welcome, and Susi, not in
the least deceived by my words, growls and barks
implacably at the intruder (when she is a little older
she will certainly bite him gently), then the little dog
is not only revealing the remarkable capacity to read
my inmost thoughts which is the heritage of Tito, but
she *is* Tito, the very personification of Tito! When in
a dry meadow she hunts mice, and dashes along in a
series of exaggerated leaps like so many mice-hunting
beasts of prey, exhibiting thereby the exaggerated
passion for this activity of her Chow ancestor, Pygi,
then she *is* Pygi. When during her training to 'lie
down' which we have been practising for some time,
she finds exactly the same hollow excuses for getting
up again which her great grandmother Stasi invented eleven years ago, and when, like the latter,
she wallows ecstatically in every puddle, and afterwards, coated in mud and slime, walks innocently
into the house, then she *is* Stasi, Stasi rediviva. And
when, along quiet riverside ways, dusty roads or city

streets, she follows in my footsteps, straining every sense not to lose me, then she is every dog, every dog that ever followed its master since the first jackal began: an immeasurable sum of love and fidelity.